"Business for Authors has now become my business bible. Packed with advice, experience and knowledge, it opened my mind to so much more that I could be doing."

Mel Sherratt, Crime writer and Amazon UK #1 Bestseller.

"With *Business for Authors*, I felt like I stepped inside the brain of an entrepreneur. I love how Joanna explored the topic from so many angles, and then provided real-life context of how she worked through each opportunity/challenge."

Dan Blank, WeGrowMedia.com

"This book demonstrates why Joanna Penn has become a favorite role model for professional author-publishers, those indie-minded writers who want to turn their passion into their job. In it Penn offers the step-by-step process she has followed to success and covers every aspect of earning a good living from writing. Not a word is wasted and not a lesson offered that hasn't been forged in the hotbed of her own experience. A must-have book for every indie author."

Orna Ross, Bestselling author and founder of the Alliance of Independent Authors

"Business for Authors ought to be required reading if you're a beginning writer who wants to make money in publishing. You can learn it all the hard way, like I did, but that usually takes years and you'll make a LOT of mistakes along the way. Or you can read through Joanna Penn's awesome little guidebook in just a few hours and save yourself a huge amount of time, energy, and money."

Randy Ingermanson, author of 'Writing Fiction for Dummies'

"This is exactly the book I needed! Business for Authors is like having a charming double agent from the world of business who can tell you all its coveted secrets. It reads like an engaging conversation with someone you can trust and along the way you learn the language and strategies of a true entrepreneur. I wish I had been given this book when I first graduated from my MFA program, back when the accounting of writing was even more of a mystery to me. With warmth and intelligence, Penn demystifies so much about what it takes to be a writer for life. This is a book that will remain on my bookshelf for years to come."

Elizabeth Hyde Stevens, Author of 'Make Art Make Money: Lessons from Jim Henson on Fueling Your Creative Career' and Lecturer at Boston University and Harvard University Extension School

"Ready to become CEO of your own Global Media Empire? Then Business for Authors is for you, featuring clear and concise steps to managing your writing career."

~New York Times and USA Today bestselling author CJ Lyons

BUSINESS

-FOR-

Authors

HOW TO BE AN
AUTHOR ENTREPRENEUR

First Edition

Joanna Penn

Business for Authors: How to be an Author Entrepreneur
First Edition (2014)

ISBN: 978-1501078330

Published by The Creative Penn Limited
www.TheCreativePenn.com

Cover Design: Derek Murphy Creativindie
www.bookcovers.creativindie.com

Interior Design: Jane Dixon Smith
www.jdsmith-design.com

Author photo credit: Mim Saxl Photography
www.mimsaxl.com

Dedicated to Julie Hall, my business accountability partner; and to Orna Ross, my creative mentor.

Thank you for your support over the last few years.

And to the readers of my books and my blog – thank you for your support. I wouldn't have this business without you!

Contents

Is this book for you?

This is not a book about the craft of writing.

I love the inexplicable process of finding ideas in the world and turning them into stories. I relish the moments of creative flow that can sometimes surprise us. Art for the sake of art is important. Writing for the love of it, or to create something beautiful on the page, is absolutely worthwhile and critical for expanding the sum of human expression. But I'm not here to talk about creativity or the craft of writing in this book.

My aim is to take the result of your creativity into the realm of actually paying the bills. To take you from being an author to running a business as an author.

In a publishing landscape that is shifting every month, authors are struggling to find the right information to survive and hopefully thrive in this new digital world. Many are scared about the fast pace of change, while still trying to navigate the new world.

I'm an author of both fiction and non-fiction, but I also spent 13 years as a business consultant in large corporates, as well as small and medium companies. I have also started a number of my own businesses and learned a lot along the way about what works and what doesn't. Now I want to introduce concepts from the business world into the author's domain.

This book is written from the perspective of an independent author, but it can also apply to those in traditional publishing who want to develop a more business-minded approach. Many authors don't consider themselves to be business people – perhaps you don't as yet. It's my aim to try to change that with this book.

Do you want your creative work to pay the bills?

If yes, read on.

Introduction

"The writer has a body, which includes a stomach.
Writers too must eat.

You can have money of your own;
you can marry money;
you can attract a patron – whether a king,
a duke, or an arts board; you can have a
day job; or you can sell to the market."

Margaret Atwood, **Negotiating with the Dead:
A Writer on Writing.**

**It's a phenomenal time to be an author ... if you change
your mindset to that of an entrepreneur.**

You are empowered to create whatever you want. You don't
have to ask permission. You don't have to compromise to
fit with anyone else's vision for your creative work. You can
write what you want, when you want and publish at your
own pace.

You can reach customers directly. You don't need anyone in
the middle. You can publish globally in multiple formats,
using freelancers to develop professional products and
help you to reach those markets.

You have freedom of creative expression. You can make
decisions about your business without consulting anyone
else. If you want to, you can work with agents and publishers who can help expand the licensing of your rights, or

you can do it yourself. You can design your life around writing books for happy readers.

This is a long-term career and it is possible to make a living as a writer. In fact, you can even make a very good living!

The world has changed … the rise of indie and artisanal

I love the term 'indie author,' as it resonates with the same energy as indie film and indie music: artists who create without big labels, who are perceived as more original than the blockbuster names. The shopping public are moving towards supporting artists directly, frequenting farmers' markets, supporting Kickstarter projects and buying direct from craftspeople online.

There's been a renaissance in people shopping for artisan-made goods, crafted with care in smaller batches. People want to shop from those who care enough to dedicate their time to making beautiful things, true artisans who put their heart and their story into their work. Guy Kawasaki coined the term 'artisanal publishing' in his book *Author, Publisher, Entrepreneur*, and it's a phrase that also resonates with indies because it implies creative freedom, and dedication to quality on a small scale.

Last Christmas, I didn't want to shop in the usual high street stores, buying soulless brand-named gifts that everyone had already seen. Instead, I bought my gifts from www.NotOnTheHighStreet.com and www.Etsy.com. On a Saturday morning, we go to our local farmers' market and buy vegetables from those who grow them, instead of buying them at the supermarket. I recently bought a coat from a leather artist in Spitalfields market, and had skirts made out of saris I bought in India by a freelance dress-maker. For my book *Desecration*, the print edition contains interior designs from an artist in the Netherlands who I found through Pinterest. I drink in bars in London where they serve strangely named beers from micro-breweries, only available locally. Has your shopping behavior changed in the same way as mine? Perhaps you can see the world changing, too.

I'm an author, just like you. I'm an artist ... and I'm a businesswoman.

I write thrillers on the edge, books that span the genres of thriller, action-adventure, and crime, with aspects of the supernatural. I also write non-fiction books for authors, like this one, as well as books on marketing and public speaking. I'm an international professional speaker and I've been a full-time author-entrepreneur since September 2011.

Before that, I spent 13 years as a business consultant, implementing financial systems into large corporates as well as small companies. I've worked in production plants with robots, on remote mining sites, and in fancy head offices with modern art on the walls. I've worked in companies where millions flowed through the accounts every day and in companies that scrutinized every penny. I've worked in companies in UK, Belgium, Finland and Holland, as well as New Zealand, Australia, and the US.

The discussion of art and money is often fraught with emotion, but I care deeply about tackling this issue.

I have a god-daughter who is 17 and making choices about her courses at University. She is being directed into subjects that will drive her into getting a 'proper' job, and away from creative courses like photography. I have a little cousin who won a creative writing competition at age 10 but is being encouraged to focus on other subjects because her parents and teachers believe that there's no career in creative writing – not one that pays well, anyway. I want to be an example to these young people. I want to be the person who proves to them that you can earn a good living as a creative.

I am also naturally ambitious, driven to succeed. I was brought up by a single mum who worked incredibly hard to put me and my brother through the best education, and who always told us that we could succeed in anything we wanted to do. We all have one life – and one chance to make it the best we can.

Authors generally aren't educated in business, focusing purely on the creative side, while tending to rely on others to do that other side of things. But business is inherently creative – by their very nature, businesses create new products, services, buildings, jobs, and wealth in the world. To be part of that creative drive can be exhilarating!

In this book, I'll be taking aspects of business and applying them to the author experience in order to empower you with the knowledge that you need to thrive in this new world of opportunity.

All companies have a similar framework, whatever their size, and in this book, I deliberately use the language of business to demonstrate that being a professional author is no different in terms of the fundamentals.

Businesses have:

- An entrepreneurial beginning and **a reason to exist** and grow: covered in Part 1.

- **Products or services** that people want to buy: covered in Part 2.

- **Employees and/or contractors** to do the work in the business, and suppliers that they pay for materials, products and services: covered in Part 3.

- **Customers** who pay money in exchange for products and services they want, as well as customer service to keep existing customers happy: covered in Part 4.

- A **distribution network** to get the products to customers, and a way to sell those products: covered in Part 5.

- **Marketing** as a way to tell more people about their products and services: covered in Part 6.

- **Financial accounting** to deal with income, expenditure, cashflow, reporting, and statutory obligations like tax: covered in Part 7.

- **Strategy, reporting and planning**, so that the company survives into the future: covered in Part 8.

Each chapter explores the topic in more detail so you can learn what's needed as well as being able to optimize your own time and energy. There are also lots of hyperlinks to online resources, which you can also find on **www.TheCreativePenn.com/businessbook-downloads.**

There you will also find a Companion Workbook with the questions from each chapter compiled into one document so you can answer them as you go through the book.

Creating things is hard work. So is running a business.

Just as you continue to learn your writing craft, you also have to learn the skills of business if you want to thrive in this new world. Let's get straight into it!

Part 1:
From Author to Entrepreneur

1.1 Arc of the author: From author to running a business as an author

When you first have a yearning to write a book, you're not usually thinking of running a global media empire! So don't worry if you're not ready to assume the mantle of CEO of your own business just yet. The aim of this book is to help you on the journey, addressing the challenges you will meet along the way.

You don't have to know everything right now. You can learn on the job. We all have to.

This is the arc of the author's writing life as I have experienced it, and the main challenges at each stage. Use the stages to assess where you are on your writer's journey.

Stage 1: "I want to write a book"

You've always been a reader and now you're reading all the 'how to' books on writing. You're attending seminars and conferences on writing. Perhaps you're writing lots already, or perhaps you're learning about writing without doing it yet. Maybe you're scared that what you write will be terrible. Maybe what you're writing is terrible. But you know you want to be a writer, and you're going to put in the effort to write that first book. You have a huge learning curve ahead, but you know you will persist.

Challenge: Actually writing and finishing a book. You can read all the books on writing, but until you actually sit down and write, you won't get black on white.

How to overcome it:

There were a couple of things that helped me at this stage:

- **The realization that 'it's OK to suck' in your first draft** (as discussed by Mur Lafferty in her podcast, I Should Be Writing and in this interview: http://bit.ly/1nvJuBv). This is also the theme of the book 'Bird by Bird' by Anne Lamott, where she advocates writing "shitty first drafts." My own metaphor for this is Michelangelo's statue of David – Michelangelo said that he saw David within the marble and he just had to cut away the excess and then polish it until it was perfect. Authors have to create the block of marble with that first draft, and then editing, rewriting and polishing will shape the statue into a masterpiece. Creating that block is a hell of a lot of work!

- **Do timed writing exercises**, in a class if you don't have the discipline to do this alone. Use Write or Die software. Set word count goals. Do National Novel Writing Month www.NaNoWriMo.org. Do anything to get a first draft done. It's hard work, people. Writing a book is not easy, otherwise everyone who says they want to write one would!

- **Go through the learning curve while actually writing**. Don't read a book on self-editing until you're actually editing. Invest in a professional editor to help you with your writing. Write a lot. You won't improve unless you write more.

- **Read self-help books around writing and mindset** and listen to podcasts/motivational audios, some of which are listed in Appendix A: Resources. Focus on shifting your mindset to that of an author.

Business readiness: It's great to be aiming for an author business at this stage, but don't get distracted by thinking too far ahead. Finish that book first! Without a product, your business is dead in the water.

Stage 2: "I am a new author"

To get to this point, you've learned the process to get from words to first draft to finished product, and you've worked with an editor to improve your book. You've learned how to self-publish, or you've made it through the process of agent and publisher. You've got the book out into the world! There are many people who say that they want to write a book but never actually get around to it, so congratulations if you now have your first book!

Challenge: Realizing that very few people actually care that you wrote a book, and that you have to learn about marketing or few people will ever read it. Realizing that you're not a millionaire and that the income from one book is not significant. Realizing that this is just the beginning.

How to overcome it:

- **Make a decision on whether there will be more books**. Was the process of writing a book worthwhile for you? Are you brimming with ideas for a new one? Are you excited about being able to reach people with your words? Are you enthusiastic about learning more?

- **Start writing the next book**. If you have the bug, the ideas will be plentiful and you'll be ready to tackle the next book. You might need a bit of a rest, but after a while, you'll get that itch again. Get writing!

- **Learn about marketing.** Unless you are one of the very few authors whose publisher will do ALL the marketing for the rest of your life, as well as for the first month, you will need to learn about marketing.

I started to learn when I had two thousand copies of my first book sitting in my house. I had thought they would sell themselves but, of course, they didn't! That started my own journey into marketing and everything that I've learned is included in my book, *How to Market a Book*.

Business readiness: If you definitely want to write more books, then it's a good time to seriously consider what you want for your writing career. Is this truly going to become a business, or a side-hustle or hobby you love?

Stage 3: "I am an established author"

Once you've written a few books, especially if they are within the same genre or category, you know approximately what you're doing. It's still hard work, but you understand the process. If you self-publish, you know the ropes and publishing takes very little time. If you have a publisher, the procedure is established and takes longer. You've got to grips with at least some aspects of marketing. You have a website and an email list. You get fan mail from readers.

Perhaps you still work a day job, and you're wondering how to take it to the next level and become a full-time writer, or perhaps you want a side business that brings in extra money.

Challenge: Balancing your time between writing more, marketing what you already have, your real life and job as well as a family. Trying to decide whether to give up your day job for the full-time writer's life, and dealing with potential conflict with family around this. You're making some money, but perhaps not quite enough to pay all the bills and have some comfort margin.

How to overcome it:

- Use a diary to **plan your writing time** and focus on becoming more organized.

- **Get clear on your brand** and what you are delivering to what customers. This will help focus what you write and produce.

- **Establish your criteria for going full-time,** e.g. income level of $2,000 a month from books before quitting the day job. Reduce your risk, e.g. downsize, save six months' income, go part time at work.

Business readiness: This book contains the information that you need at this level to move into running a business.

Stage 4: "I am the CEO of my creative company"

There is a tipping point where you go from being an author to running a business as an author. You've decided you want to earn a full-time income from your writing, which means taking the business side seriously instead of your writing being a hobby. The penny has dropped around rights exploitation and you realize how far your work can go through the opportunities available to authors now.

Whatever the catalyst, you decide to take full control of your financial destiny and career as an author. This may mean that you go full time as an author-entrepreneur, or that you allocate a proper chunk of time to the business.

This is not a hobby anymore. To step into this phase means that you are serious about being an author-entrepreneur. You assume the CEO role – you're in charge.

Challenge: Juggling the writing, marketing, and production side, as well as trying to think about strategy, release schedules, and more. There's also your family life and your own health to consider. Trying to keep track of all your products, the rights you want to exploit, the multiple projects you have going at once, and keeping an eye on other opportunities.

How to overcome it: Read on!

1.2 Definition of an author-entrepreneur

"All humans are entrepreneurs, not because they should start companies, but because the will to create is encoded in human DNA."

Reid Hoffman, LinkedIn co-founder

An entrepreneur creates value from ideas

Ideas on their own are worthless, and creatives know this. We know that the real value is in the execution. The same idea can be turned into many different things in the mind and hands of different people. There is no one way to express an idea, which is why we don't worry about people stealing our ideas.

A writer is someone who writes.

An author is someone who writes a book, however that is defined.

An author-entrepreneur takes that book much further, exploiting the multiple opportunities and value in one manuscript and creating a viable business from the ideas in their head. (How cool is that!)

Here are some of the facets of an author-entrepreneur. Remember, **you can grow into these over time** if you don't feel ready to embrace the term entrepreneur just yet.

An author-entrepreneur loves business as well as art

We create art. We manifest our ideas in the world in glorious creative ways, but to be entrepreneurial is to care about the business side as well as about creation. It's about being excited to generate something new and original, but also being enthusiastic about how the book will reach customers as well as the financial side.

Some say that business is the ultimate creativity. You are potentially creating something huge in the world from nothing more than the human mind. Wow!

An author-entrepreneur turns one manuscript into multiple streams of income

You do not have just one book when you finish a manuscript. You have the potential to create multiple streams of income. I go into this in more detail in Part 2, but essentially you can create an ebook, a print book, and an audiobook from this one manuscript. You will likely create that in your first language, let's assume English, and you can sell those products in every country in the world. You can also sell the translation rights to any other language in the world and publish internationally, too. You can exploit film, media and other subsidiary rights as well. That's the magic of publishing!

An author-entrepreneur cares about all aspects of business

Writing and publishing are only some aspects of this entrepreneurial life. To be entrepreneurial is to understand the rest of it and make conscious choices as to how you want to publish and sell your work.

For example, it is fine to work with a literary agent, but you must understand what they are doing for their 15% of royalties for the rest of the life of the book, potentially for the rest of your life. It is fine to want help with contracts, but you should also understand for yourself what the clauses mean, so you are not signing away rights that you want to keep, or limiting your choices. It is fine to want a traditional deal, but you should understand the pros and cons of signing away your rights, and the likelihood of achieving your dreams this way.

It's understanding that a business is about sales and marketing as well as product creation, it's about failure as well as success, it's about doing the accounting and taxation aspects, as well as the conferences, speaking, and book launches. Yes, you have people to help you, but you're still the CEO, and you need to understand how it all works together.

An author-entrepreneur is empowered

Entrepreneurs don't wait for permission. They create and get their ideas into the world, and they move fast. They are empowered.

I will never forget speaking at a particular publishing conference on a panel of agents and publishers. Afterwards, a prominent UK agent said to me, "It's good to meet an author who's not so grateful."

The power differential between agents, publishers and authors has been skewed for a long time. The mere act of query and rejection makes the author increasingly desperate and then grateful to sign any kind of contract, even one that isn't in their best interests. Authors act as if the agent and publisher are doing them a favor by publishing them. But they are not running a charity. Publishing is a business that aims to make money. That's why they want your book.

An author-entrepreneur tries new things, accepts failure and pivots when necessary

Business people know that lots of things fail, and that's not a bad thing. It's just part of learning. Writing a book will never be a catastrophic failure, as you will have spent time writing, which is worthwhile in itself. But if a series just doesn't take off, then write something else. If your covers aren't attracting the right customers, change them. If you're not selling any books, learn some marketing. If you're overwhelmed with everything, prioritize and stop some of what you're doing. I've made a lot of mistakes in my business journey, but that's the way we learn. We get better by continuing to try.

An author-entrepreneur invests in themselves

The publishing industry is changing every week in this amazing time of flux, and staying up to date with new opportunities is part of the game. If you love learning, then the life of an author-entrepreneur is fantastic!

There are always new people to learn from, new things to try, new books to read, new podcasts to listen to. There's no excuse anymore for not knowing what is going on, and you should be investing money in yourself to expand your own knowledge and skills. I've listed some of these in Appendix A: Resources and I also share new things every day on Twitter @thecreativepenn.

An author-entrepreneur understands that luck plays a part

For every Facebook or Twitter, Apple or Google, there are hundreds of thousands of companies that either failed and disappeared, or that exist in the mid-list making decent money and being happy.

The stratospheric success of some books over others is a similar thing. Sometimes a book is just in the right place at the right time and hits a zeitgeist that resonates with readers. But you can't plan a stratospheric bestseller like *Harry Potter, The Da Vinci Code, 50 Shades of Grey* or *Gone Girl*, otherwise publishers would manage it with every book. You just have to try your best and see whether Lady Luck is smiling today.

For more on how to increase your luck and harness randomness, read *The Click Moment* by Frans Johansson.

An author-entrepreneur understands that the customer is critical

Yes, of course you should write the book that is in your heart. But if you want to have a business, you also have to focus on the customer. An entrepreneur knows that if they produce something that no one wants, then their business fails very fast. But if they can tap into a desire the customer has, or may not even know they have yet, then they will do amazingly well.

Let's take the Kindle, for example. I was one of those people who said that I loved print books and would never read digitally. Ebooks seemed anathema to the girl who studied in the Radcliffe Camera at Oxford University and haunted the library stacks daily in search of theological gems. I collected books from a young age and shipped over two thousand books from England to New Zealand and then on to Australia as I moved. But the price of new fiction in Australia drove me to the Kindle when it first came out, and I was hooked. My reading consumption radically exploded, from under five books a month up to three plus books a week, and I began to read a much higher percentage of fiction because I could now afford it.

Amazon understood their ideal customer for the Kindle to be the addicted super-reader, and they hooked me early. I left those two thousand print books behind in Australia, mostly giving them away in a huge garage sale. I now read 99% digitally and what I ultimately want as a consumer of books is:

- Entertainment (fiction) or education/inspiration (non-fiction)

- Unlimited choice

- Ease and speed of purchase

- Prices that enable me to consume at the rate I do and not break the bank

The model is the same for film, TV, music, and gaming, and companies have grown to fill the market. As an author-entrepreneur, I can now tap into those same consumer desires and provide content for customers like me. There's no need to reinvent the business model if you can create products that customers want. That's what we do as authors.

An author-entrepreneur believes in abundance and generosity

Generosity fosters more of the same online, and there is no zero sum game in my world. If I sell a book, it doesn't take a sale away from you. In fact, if we write in the same genre, then we should be promoting each other, as one writer can never satisfy the consumption habits of an avid fan of the genre! The number of readers is expanding as digital and mobile reading go global. We live in an abundant world.

An author-entrepreneur has a long-term view

Writing books is not a get-rich-quick scheme – it is a way of living and earning money until the day you die, and then some, as copyright extends 70 years after the death of the author, so your heirs can continue to earn from your estate. You don't write a book for next week's sales spikes; you don't jeopardize your long-term business over something ephemeral. The author-entrepreneur takes the long-term view, plans accordingly, and thinks ahead.

Are you an author-entrepreneur according to this list? Would you like to be?

1.3 What is your definition of success?

This book is intended to help you to make some decisions about your life as an author. But before you go on, you need to think about three questions:

- What is your definition of success – for this particular book and for your writing career?

- How will you track and measure that success?

- What do you want to do with that success? What is the point in your work?

One of the inherent parts of being human is a general dissatisfaction with where we are. However much we achieve, we often want more. This has an evolutionary benefit, as it means that we are always striving, always creating, always building. But it's also important to recognize your achievements, so whatever you decide you want, you also need to establish how you will measure this success.

Your definition of success will also change over time, as it is dependent on the progression of your writing career, and where you are in the arc of the author-entrepreneur. Here are some common definitions, as well as potential options for measurement.

(1) I want to create something I'm proud of and hold my book in my hand

Perhaps we all start with the desire to finish a project and create something tangible. This is also why most first-time authors want a printed book. An income goal is not necessary for everyone, and for many, creativity alone is the reward.

I helped my 9 year old niece to publish her first book, which led her to win national prizes speaking publicly about the experience. I also helped my Dad with his historical thriller, Nada. Neither of these are really commercial prospects, so the focus of success is more on creativity, which is a totally brilliant reason to write a book, but probably not why you're reading this one!

(2) I want to see my book on the shelves of a bookstore

We have shopped in bookstores all our lives and for many of us, the bookstore is a place of solace as well as adventure. When I was most miserable in my consulting job, I would go to the bookstore at lunchtime and indulge in retail therapy to escape my life for a while. To see a book with our name on it on those shelves must surely be part of every author's dream.

This is easy to measure, but it is still difficult to get into bookstores as an independent author. It's also costly, even if you can manage it, because of discounting and returns.

You can definitely do it – as Dean Wesley Smith explains in this article - http://bit.ly/1ql6mse. It's also possible to build relationships with your local bookstore, as Karen Inglis, children's author, has done - http://bit.ly/1m7kcs6. But it's about where you want to spend your energy and, for me, print distribution is not a major concern. I'll admit that this is still a dream of mine, and I'm definitely open to deals with traditional publishing, but it is no longer a definition of my own success.

(3) I want to reach readers with my words

This is fantastic, but I always challenge this definition of success because it is so intangible. If you want to reach readers, then just put your book out for free and on every platform in the world, as Seth Godin did with The IdeaVirus a few years ago. But most people don't mean this kind of 'reach.'

So, be more specific. Does it mean 10 five-star reviews on Amazon? Does it mean fan email from a reader you have never met and who isn't your friend or family member? Or should you measure this reach in book sales?

(4) I want to sell 10,000 copies of my book/s

This is a better definition than (3) because it is measurable and you know when you get there. The number is obviously dependent on many things, for example, the genre you write in, as a children's picture book will sell far fewer copies than a commercial romance novel, and a literary novel will generally sell less than a thriller. It is also dependent on how many books you have, as you will more easily reach higher figures with more books.

This volume type of definition will also change over time. I started off with 1,000 books as a goal when I only had one book. Then I moved to 10,000, then 100,000, and now my goals have changed again.

(5) I want to win a prize and receive literary/critical acclaim

You can achieve this as an independent author. The Alliance of Independent Authors has an Open Up To Indies campaign, which will hopefully mean that more prizes and festivals are open to self-published books over time. There's also been the success of *A Naked Singularity* by Sergio de la Pava, which started out as self-published, won the PEN/Robert W. Bingham prize, and was then shortlisted for the Folio prize.

But you're still far more likely to win a literary prize if you go through the traditional publishing route. It's the goal of most MFA programs to produce books capable of winning prizes. As for critical acclaim, again, you're more likely to get that through traditional publishing and reviews in literary journals.

If this is your goal, you should also be aware of recent research that shows literary prizes can make the book less popular - http://bit.ly/1gnKqV3. So this definition of success may be incompatible with making a full-time living as an author.

(6) I want to make a full-time living with my writing

Again, I challenge this, because the definition of 'full-time living' is different by country, even by region, as well as needing to take into account the huge difference between income needs from a family with kids to a professional couple or single writer.

Try to be specific about the actual figure you are aiming for, and think about how that may change over time, based on how much you are writing over the next few years, as well as your own financial requirements. This will help to guide your thought processes as you go through the rest of the book.

(7) I want to create a body of work that I am proud of over my lifetime

This is the definition that will keep you honest about your creative output. You won't rush a book to publication. You won't put a book out without a professional edit, or a professional cover. You will strive for the best this particular project can be.

I am trying to balance this with (6) above, and it can be difficult. Part of me wants to learn to write faster and produce more words, but my books are characterized by deep research and a sense of place, both of which require a longer writing process. I also want to live a life of research and travel, so I want to honor that part of my process.

In the end, I want to write for the rest of my life, hopefully another 50 years, so I'm in this for the long haul. What about you?

> "You have the right to your labor,
> not to the fruits of your labor."
>
> *Krishna*

1.4 What do you want with your life?

It was the first day of my first grown-up job after graduation. I was an analyst at Andersen Consulting (now Accenture), having left Oxford University with a degree in Theology. The room was filled with several hundred bright young things, all eager to start this new life. As the hubbub of chat died down, an HR manager put her arm out, stretching it down the middle of the room.

"Everyone on my left, you're doing SAP."

I was sitting on her left, and the following week I was in Chicago, learning SAP, an enterprise computer system that helps companies to run everything in an integrated manner. It was 1997 and we were focusing on implementing computer systems to stop the 'millennium bug.' (Remember that?)

It was 2011 before I finally gave up SAP for good, after a lot of resignations, company startups, and global moves. I used to wonder how I ended up being such an expert, when I had never intended to go down that route. A series of small, seemingly insignificant decisions led to that point. Like me, many people fall into a day job, and wonder how they got there years later.

Don't let that happen to your writing career. Make active decisions that will guide your journey.

The previous section focused on the specifics of success around your writing, and your books – but that can be too narrow a focus when you consider starting a business. There is no set path on the road to entrepreneurship. There are models and there are opinions, but you will have to find your own way through the maze of decisions. Here are some questions that can help you.

What do you want your life to be like?

The decisions that you make about your business can affect everything else, so if you decide upfront how to design your life, your decisions about business will follow more easily. You can also weigh up the pros and cons of each situation based on your overarching life goals.

Here are some examples:

Life decision: Spend more time with family.

This might mean that you decide to work at home in order to see your children before school and be around for them before bedtime. This is fantastic, but you'll need to make sure you can work flexibly. Writing is actually a great job for this, but many writers have to shut their doors and keep the children out in order to get anything done, or write in the hours when the children are asleep.

Life decision: Location independence.

You want to be able to work from anywhere in the world. You want to be able to travel and move when you like, and not be tied down by mortgage or an accumulation of 'things and stuff.'

Notice how neither of these mention income goals. That's because money alone is not the point. The point is how you want your life to be.

In the first example, that person would likely take more time with their family over more money. In the second example, location independence means that you can move somewhere cheaper to live, so quality of life is relative.

What is non-negotiable for you?

You also have to define your boundaries and what is non-negotiable. What are you unwilling to live without? What won't you compromise on? Non-negotiable for you may include a house (rent/mortgage) and good schools for your kids, healthcare, and a car. Your boundaries may include protecting the privacy of your family.

I enjoy location independence and the ability to travel, and for that, I have given up the stability of owning a house, furniture and a car. For me, the boundaries on my creativity are the important ones. I'm a businesswoman, but I will only write things that I love to write and that I feel add to my body of work in the world. I also have a boundary around protecting my husband's privacy, so our digital lives are very separate and we don't share a surname.

What are your core values?

This is hard to do, but try to distill your values down to one word that can help you make decisions about your business. Assume that love is included as a default, so you're not allowed to use that!

Here are some examples:

Loyalty. This is what an author friend of mine said after much consideration recently. This spills over into relationships and business agreements with people, even when it might not turn out to her advantage. She values the loyalty aspect more than the financial, and that's to be respected. She's also loyal to her readers, holding to the structure and genre of what they enjoy reading.

Freedom. This is my word, and one that took me many years to figure out. It's not being lonely, as I'm happily married and have good friends. But it's why I choose not to own property or a car, or even any furniture (I rent it). It's why I have no debt, no mortgage, no financial ties. I choose location independence. I choose to be an independent author as I don't like being locked into one path. I don't like asking permission! This guides my decisions around not wanting physical stock, around using professionals all over the world rather than physically near me, around doing most of my business in US dollars, and marketing to a global audience online rather than focusing on local impact.

Peace. I have a friend who has a chronic physical illness and so she seeks peace as a primary value. She would rather have a publisher or agent handle the business side and take it off her hands. She's happy to pay a premium for that.

Hopefully these questions will give you a framework for thinking about your life and your author business in a wider context than just the next book and the next few years.

1.5 Should you start a company?

I'm covering this up-front because I know it's a question many authors have.

IMPORTANT: *I'm not a lawyer, an accountant or a business advisor, so this is not business advice! This is just my opinion and it doesn't go into great detail as this is a very tricky area that needs expert advice to navigate. I'm based in the UK, so the terminology and details will differ per country, although the principles generally remain the same wherever you are.*

Many authors have other jobs, and the income from books usually starts off small, so the question of whether to start a company is often considered later in an author's career. Here are some fundamentals:

- **You don't need to have a company legal entity (or whatever it is called in your country) set up in order to write, publish and sell books.** You can just start doing this under your personal name, and if you want, you can set up a company later. So there's no rush, and in fact, it's much better to take your time about the decision because of the responsibilities that go with company setup. Many people who write one book don't go on to write another, so you need to be sure that this is what you want to do before you commit.

- **You will need to pay the appropriate income tax** for your country on any money you receive from book sales/royalties from publishers. If you have a company, this will go through your company accounts, but if you don't, you will need to account for the extra income on your personal tax return.

- You can set up a **separate bank account** for your author business without starting a legal company. It's a good idea to do this, as then you can at least track your income and expenses at a more granular level. You can enter the bank account details into the publishing systems so that your income is paid to this account.

- **The author name you publish under does not need to relate to the company name or your personal name**. When you self-publish, there are different fields for the author name versus the legal side of things, and traditional publishers are used to handling this for you as well.

- **You can also publish under an imprint** or publisher name that you decide to use, without needing to set up a legal company for this imprint. There are four separate fields in the various self-publishing systems: your name for the account, your author name per book, your legal name for the tax returns (company name or personal name) and your publisher name (which doesn't have to be a company).

So, you can do pretty much everything under your own name, as a sole trader, as long as you report the income. When should you consider investigating whether to start your own company?

There are various legal structures that can be used for different situations, for example, a Sole Trader or Partnership is a different setup to a Limited Company in the UK. If you're co-writing over the long term, then you might consider a different business structure for assets created together, as opposed to your own work. These structures will also differ per country, so you will need to ask for professional advice locally for your specific situation.

All structures have a greater responsibility than individuals trading under their own name, for example:

- Keeping accurate records of company business

- Keeping financial accounts and filing annual company statements

- Statutory reporting to the company and tax authorities

You will also need to pay for setup as well as ongoing management of the company, so there are more costs involved, and sometimes these can be significant. You'll need a new bank account and it's advisable to have an accountant and tax agent as well. It's not a simple endeavor, that's for sure, so it is a personal decision.

Why I choose to use a company structure for my own business

I personally choose to operate my author-entrepreneur business as a UK limited company, The Creative Penn Limited. I have started a number of companies in various structures over the last ten years. I had one in Australia for my author/speaker business and another for property investment. I also had several in New Zealand, so using a company structure is within my comfort zone. It might seem scary if it's not something you're used to, but once you've spent a few hours reading all the documentation and talking with a professional, you won't find it so daunting.

I started a limited company as soon as I moved back to the UK in May 2011 for these reasons:

- **Taking this career seriously.** The company is responsible in its own right and its finances are separate to mine. I have to put my business owner's hat on when I consider my time and responsibilities and having to report on financial accounts and the status of the company every year helps to keep me focused.

- **Planning for success.** There are various financial efficiencies that a business can use. The company does its accounts, pays corporation tax and then allocates profits. I went into this business assuming that my profits will grow over time, and that having them within a company structure is the best long term. If you look at the top-earning authors, you will find that they have some kind of legal structure in place. The question is more about when you set this up.

- **Asset protection**. Some structures can protect what you personally own from potential litigation. This is a complicated legal area and again I'm not qualified to comment on the detail. But essentially, anything I own personally or with my husband, is separate from what is held within the company.

- **Estate planning**. A company functions entirely separately from the individuals, and when I die, it can be run without me and continue to provide income for shareholders through my assets. For more on estate planning and its importance, read this series of articles by Kristine Kathryn Rusch - http://bit.ly/1tr55lp.

So, I am personally happy to go through the initial setup pain and the ongoing costs of doing business under a company structure in order to have these advantages. But you have to make a decision for your own situation which, of course, will change over time. If you do decide to go forward, setting up a company is not too complicated. The following resources will help.

Resources: for US, UK and Canada

- Starting a new business in the US -
  http://1.usa.gov/1ghKyXA

- Starting a new business in the UK –
  http://hmrc.gov.uk/startingup

- Starting a new business in Canada -
  http://bit.ly/1ruaTqg

For other countries, just search for 'starting a new business'
+ your country.

Part 2: Products and Services

2.1 Definition

"Every successful business creates or provides something of value that other people want or need, at a price they're willing to pay, that satisfies the purchaser's needs and expectations and that provides the business sufficient revenue to make it worthwhile for the owners to continue operation."

Josh Kaufman, **The Personal MBA**

Art for the sake of art is important – but you need to shift your mindset if you want to run a business. You need to sell something in order to make money.

In this section, we explore the various products that your author business can produce, as well as some details on contracts, copyright, and piracy. We evaluate business models for authors as well as how you can assess your own ideas, and how to put together a production plan to take your business to the next level.

2.2 It's not just one book. Your rights and how to exploit them

Warning: this may blow your mind! It blew mine when the penny finally dropped on what this truly means for my lifetime creative opportunities.

The magic of scalable income

Scalability is a key concept for creatives, and it is pretty exciting for authors. It means that you create something once and then you sell it multiple times. For our purposes, the book is the perfect example of the scalable product. You can write a manuscript, and then turn it into an ebook, print book, and audiobook in English and whichever other languages you can sell. Then those products sell multiple times, earning income on every copy. So you write it once and it can earn you money for the rest of your life and, thanks to copyright law, seventy years after your death. It's scalable because the effort is put in once and the return just keeps on coming.

Time-based income is your day job, or professional speaking or anything that pays once and is constrained by your physical presence. We only have a finite amount of time on this earth, so time is our most precious resource. You can use your time to be paid once for the work, or to create something that will sell over and over again. Most of us need to have a balance at the beginning, as we need immediate cash flow to pay the bills, but think about your time as precious every time you sit down to work. Is what you're doing scalable?

The diagram below outlines the rights model as I see it today. *Disclaimer: I am not a lawyer and this is not legal, contractual or financial advice. It is just my opinion and I can't answer any legal or financial questions.*

Value your work

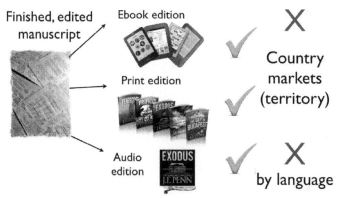

Finished, edited manuscript

Ebook edition

Print edition

Audio edition

✓ X Country markets (territory)

✓ X by language

Plus/ other subsidiary rights

Your manuscript starts as just one document.

Because of this, authors generally think in terms of one book and they don't even realize that multiple streams of income can flow from this small beginning. Yes, it's just one manuscript but you can turn that one book into multiple products.

[Note: This is not a book on how to self-publish. I recommend *Let's Get Digital* by David Gaughran, and *Choosing a Self-Publishing Service* by the Alliance of Independent Authors. There's also a round-up on my site here - http://bit.ly/1lGihkh]

(1) Ebooks

The main file types are mobi (for Kindle), ePub (for most other devices), PDF (for reading on computers). You can create these yourself using tools like Scrivener or pay for conversion services. You can then sell these files on multiple devices: Kindle, Kobo, Nook, Apple devices, cell-phones through apps, as well as online through websites. This alone ends up giving you multiple income streams as the indie author is paid from each store separately.

(2) Print

Print-on-demand technology means that you don't have to pay upfront or warehouse and ship physical products anymore. You can use services like Createspace, Ingram Spark, or LightningSource to upload files and have your print books available for sale online through Amazon, Barnes & Noble, and many other online bookstores. When a customer orders the book, one copy is printed and sent directly to them, and you receive whatever profit margin you set up. You can also do short runs if you have a distribution model.

(3) Audio

With many workers commuting for hours every day, and the ease of using digital audio files, audiobooks are an expanding market. Your books can be made available for sale through Audible, iTunes, Brilliance and other services. For indie authors in some countries, ACX.com is a great way to get your books into audio format using royalty share deals, and hopefully this will be expanding to other markets over time.

So that's already one manuscript into three products ... but it gets better!

(4) Multiply these editions by country markets, which come under the heading 'territory' in publishing contracts

Through Amazon, Kobo, iBookstore and NookPress, as well as through distributors like Smashwords, you can reach multiple territories yourself. The Kobo Writing Life platform even has a fantastic world map so you can see where people have purchased your books. I've now sold books in 58 countries, including such diverse places as Ecuador, Burkina Faso, Nepal, and Iceland. Now that's exciting! Although the volume is quite large in the more mature markets, most of those country sales are small right now. But that's because the online book sales markets are only just beginning in the global markets.

Fast forward a few years and I think you'll see how different things will be. The story in the last few years has been about the maturing US/UK/Canadian digital market, but over the next few years, the focus will be on the rest of the world. If you own your rights, you have the potential to sell your products all over the world, with more territories getting into digital books every month.

(5) Multiply these editions by language

Spanish is the second most commonly spoken language in the world after Mandarin, with over 400 million native speakers. For the ebook market specifically, Spanish is the second most commonly spoken language in the US, which is the most mature ebook market. There are also specific ebook stores for Spain and emerging markets in the South American countries.

Germany has a population of 80 million, but the book sales volume is 40% of the USA's (against a population of 300m) so the Germans are big readers. There are also German speakers in Austria, Switzerland and, of course, the rest of the world. Ebook adoption is increasing and Germany is the third largest ebook market after the US and UK. Those are just two examples of opportunities for expanding your work into other languages and reaching new readers. The sales may be small initially but with a longer-term view, it's likely to only get better.

You can use an agent to find foreign rights deals for you. Yes, you will have to pay the percentage agreed, but it does mean that you have someone else working on your behalf. In terms of what an agent will take for these kind of deals, it will depend on whether they use sub-agents per country. It's usually 15% for one agent or 20% for two in a sub-agent situation, splitting the deal between them at 10% each.

There are now a couple of sites that you can use to sell your own foreign rights: IPR License and PubMatch. Both sites include the opportunity to upload your books, search the database for publishers matching your requirements, and the ability to pitch. You can also pitch publishers directly, especially in countries where agents are used less than the US and UK. If your books do really well and you become more visible as an indie author, you are likely to get approached directly anyway.

There are a couple of options for doing this yourself. You can source translators and pay them upfront so that you retain 100% of rights, then publish on the various country-specific platforms. This requires an investment to pay the translator as well as knowledge of each country, and with language issues, this can be a challenge.

You can also do joint-venture deals with translators, offering them a royalty share for their work. I have a number of 50:50 royalty share partnerships with translators, where they are also marketing partners, incentivized by the possibility of higher royalties. This means that we both get ongoing income, but I haven't paid upfront for any translation, similar to the ACX model for audiobooks.

I also get the benefit of a language specialist and someone in the country to translate extra marketing materials e.g. a newsletter in a specific language. Clearly, this is a risk for both parties, but a translator will generally only consider this for an author with a good sales history and an established platform. Here's my own experience of self-publishing in translation with plus interviews with my Spanish, Italian and German translators - http://bit.ly/1lcdKW5.

The rewards of doing it yourself include higher royalties and more control over pricing, the same as any kind of self-publishing. The challenges are greater as you expand the number of countries in which you operate, as you will be dealing with different publishing platforms, different languages and an expanding number of translation partners that you have to manage as well as pay monthly. My own approach is to do a limited number of these deals in major languages to test the market.

Other subsidiary rights

There are also opportunities for other subsidiary rights. For example, I sold some short stories to Kobo, which they used for the launch of Dan Brown's *Inferno* and then for an exclusive period. But after six months, I got the rights back and published *A Thousand Fiendish Angels* as a free short story collection.

You can also turn your non-fiction book into a multimedia product with video and audio that sells for more money than a book. But I absolutely acknowledge that some rights are hard to exploit without expert knowledge. Film and TV rights, for example, are not something that most indies are getting into yet, although again, indie author Hugh Howey managed to attract Ridley Scott with *Wool*, negotiating rights through his agent. There really are no rules!

When should you sell your rights?

It's completely up to you. As the CEO of your business, you get to decide what's best for your creative project.

The position of many professional indie authors these days seems to be more about partnership with publishers on rights deals that are good for both parties. Hugh Howey and others have taken print-only deals in English, keeping their ebook and audiobook rights. I've taken an ebook-only deal in German, something I wouldn't do in English, as more of a marketing play. I also did an audio-only deal in the US before ACX was available for UK authors.

I would definitely consider any print-only deal, as well as foreign language deals, in order to get into new markets. For example, I'd love to have my books available in Mandarin and Arabic, which together encompass a huge market worldwide. I also have my heart set on India as a key market, as I love the country and need an excuse to go more often! But for me, any contractual discussion must be about partnership.

The main thing to remember is that the publishing business is not a charity. Your work is valuable.

Don't give up your rights easily and make sure it's the best deal for you long term.

Publishing companies are interested in making money, and your manuscript enables them to do that. So if you want to sign with an agent or a publisher, go ahead, but know what you're doing. If you're an indie, I hope this excites you about the possibilities, because the road ahead is tremendously exciting!

2.3 Business models for authors

Many authors have day jobs, which is a great way to pay the bills, with writing being just for fun or extra income, but this is aimed at authors who are intent on going full time in the business.

Why do you need to define your business model?

Defining your business model can help to keep you focused. Opportunities expand as your profile grows, and keeping your business model foremost in your mind can help you to say no to things that distract you. *[I need to remind myself of this all the time!]*

For example, renowned indie author JA Konrath states, "I gave up on public appearances a few years ago, because of diminishing returns. They were indeed fun, but the cost and time away from writing wasn't worth it to me."

These are the most common business models for author-entrepreneurs and you can, of course, mix and match between them.

Business model 1: Non-fiction books with multimedia products, speaking and consulting

Many non-fiction authors make more money from the 'back-end' of their books than from book sales alone. This includes information product sales, professional speaking and consulting/coaching services. The book acts more as a business card as well as providing qualified leads and status for the author. The book itself doesn't need to make any money – it's the other services you make available that are more important for cashflow.

Big-name speakers like Anthony Robbins, Robert Kiyosaki and Jack Canfield are examples in which the back-end business is worth far more than the book sales. Recently, the Wolf of Wall Street, Jordan Belfort has started to use this model. He wrote the bestselling book that became the film while he was in prison, and is reportedly set to earn $100 million from speaking events and course sales in 2014. He has said that he makes more from this new business model than he did from stock trading. Of course, that's an extreme example, and you may disagree with his ethics – but it's a good example of how the business model works.

A more authentic example is Chris Brogan, author of *The Freaks Shall Inherit the Earth*, and other books. Chris is a highly paid professional speaker, and consults for large corporates on marketing, as well as producing *Owner* magazine and online training courses for bloggers. In terms of indies, Jim Kukral of Author Marketing Club also primarily uses this model, providing author services, consulting and professional speaking as well as writing non-fiction books.

You can also include those authors who write non-fiction books for writers. For example, SARK, of the wildly colorful creativity books, has online courses, as does Julia Cameron from The Artist's Way. Robert McKee, who wrote the must-read craft book, *Story*, has an extensive online video membership program, as well as running multi-day speaking events for premium prices.

So, if you're writing non-fiction, consider how you can turn that into other products to offer more to your customers.

Authors of non-fiction often have online businesses which facilitate the use of other income options:

- **Advertising.** People pay you to promote their work on your site. This might be a banner ad, or a sponsored article. You generally need to have a popular website for people to pay for this type of thing.

- **Affiliate income.** You receive a percentage of a sale when someone buys a product/service from someone else. I like this model and use it extensively on my website for products and services I use myself. For example, I'm an affiliate for Amazon, Learn Scrivener Fast training, Author Marketing Club and Book Design Templates, all of which I use myself and therefore recommend. Again, you need an established audience and popular website for this type of income to be significant.

- **Author services.** There are many authors who are now supporting the industry by putting their new-found skills to work. Many ebook formatters, editors and cover designers are also authors, supplementing their income by sharing their expertise.

Business model 2:
High-volume book releases

For self-published or hybrid authors, the model of writing fast and publishing often has become mainstream in the last few years.

It's not a new model, as it reflects the way the pulp writers of the early 1900s wrote, producing massive amounts of escapist fiction which was printed on cheap 'pulp' paper so that the price could be kept low. *[It does not mean the writing was bad!]*

Readers ate it up like candy, and authors became well known.

This same phenomenon has emerged since ebooks went mainstream. A good indie fiction example is H.M. Ward, who releases romance novellas every few weeks and has sold over 4 million books, as well as hitting the New York Times bestseller list 11 times in 2013. In non-fiction, author Steve Scott releases a book a month, and with over 40 titles, his monthly income from book sales alone is significant.

Some authors are achieving this volume through collaboration, for example Sean Platt writes with David Wright and separately writes with Johnny B. Truant to produce books under the Sterling and Stone brand. Together, they produce an enormously varied number of series and a lot of books a year.

This is not just an indie author model.

Isaac Asimov wrote over 500 books in his lifetime, Enid Blyton wrote over 600, Barbara Cartland over 700. Prolific authors still creating at a ferocious pace for their traditional publishers include R. L. Stine, the bestselling children's author of all time, who has been known to write several books a month. There's also Nora Roberts, who also writes under J.D. Robb, and who writes a book every 45 days, writing eight hours a day.

Business model 3: Sporadic books with teaching/speaking/freelance writing

Of course, not everyone wants to write books at such a prolific pace, and literary writers in particular don't work this fast. More attention is paid to the language than keeping the reader enthralled in the plot. Therefore, it's rare for a literary writer to make a full-time income from book sales alone, unless that book happens to win a major prize.

So the business model for literary writers is usually to combine writing with teaching creative writing, applying for grants and prizes, or with another writing career like journalism or freelance writing. If you take a look at the prestigious Iowa Writer's Workshop faculty, you will see famous literary writers and poets like Simon Armitage, Ian McEwan, John Irving and more, who make money through teaching as well as writing.

What business model are you aiming for?

These business models can be mixed and matched, and my own is a combination of all of these right now. I receive income from the sales of fiction and non-fiction books, from the sale of online training courses, professional speaking and also affiliate income from my blog. There are no rules and this is a mix'n'match game!

But if you want to be a full-time author, you need to consider how your income streams will work. You need some model to follow, and it's unlikely that a full-time income will be based on only one thing.

2.4 Evaluating business models

There are several ways to evaluate a market, as outlined in Josh Kaufman's *Personal MBA* book, which goes into an assessment of whether a business idea should be investigated further. I've taken his concepts and applied them to the business of being an indie author in order to help prove the concept.

Kaufman suggests that you rate each of the following sections from 0 to 10, where 0 is extremely unattractive and 10 is extremely attractive. I've entered my scores based on writing thrillers as an indie author, but the numbers may be different for your author business. You can choose to consider what you do now, or what you intend to do in the future. It's important to think about your business model in this critical way in order to evaluate its business potential.

(1) Urgency. How badly do people want or need this right now?

People only desperately want a book if their information need is immediate (generally non-fiction), or they are about to get on a plane with nothing to read, or if there is a 'must-read' book that everyone is talking about e.g. *50 Shades of Grey*. But in general, books are not an urgent purchase.

Score: 1

(2) Market Size. How many people are actively purchasing things like this?

I don't have the latest figures, but the market for books worldwide is certainly in the billions of dollars. The question is, how does that break down for your type of book? For example, compare a romance novel ebook selling on Amazon in English with a poetry chapbook in Dutch selling in a unique bookstore in a chic corner of Amsterdam.

So, think about the market for your book/s in multiple dimensions:

- Genre – big sellers like romance, sci-fi/fantasy, mystery/thriller vs. lit fic or poetry. AuthorEarnings.com has a done a great job of giving the data behind the assumptions per genre.

- Format – ebook, print, audio

- Distribution platforms – the big ones are obviously Amazon, iBooks, Kobo, Nook but there are also country-specific platforms.

- Language – English is the biggest seller and sold in the most countries, with the US and UK being the biggest markets. In Europe, German is the next biggest language seller for indies, with Spanish coming next. Although Mandarin and Arabic books would reach a lot of people, indie authors don't yet have platforms to reach that segment.

One of my pet peeves is when authors say, "My book is so original that it doesn't fit any categories." Clearly, if it doesn't fit any category in the biggest bookstore in the world, then it's unlikely that there's a market for it, or at least only a very small one. You have to look at the most popular categories on Amazon in order to assess the potential market size.

Score: 8 – for mystery/thrillers, the genre in which I write fiction.

(3) Pricing potential. What is the highest price people will pay for this type of product?

With books, we are at the lower end of the scale. I read 99% on the Kindle and I prefer to pay under £10 for a book, preferably under £5. The most I have paid for a book was ~£100 for the oversize, full color edition of Carl Jung's *Red Book*. Personalized, limited edition hardbacks for super-fans may command higher prices, for example, Cory Doctorow's hand-bound, hardcover of *With a Little Help* for $275. But we all know that books are a commodity game – we price low, and we need to sell in bulk to make decent money.

If you write non-fiction and have higher priced back-end products, you will have better pricing options.

Score: 2. Prices are low in general.

(4) Cost of customer acquisition. How easy is it to acquire a new customer? How much will it cost to generate a sale?

This is an interesting question, because most indies sell through established retailers like Amazon, Kobo, iBooks and Nook who already have customers. The difficulty is getting the customer onto our own book sales page, and this is generally achieved through marketing activities. Most indie authors use free and low-cost marketing tactics, and occasionally spend a few hundred dollars on BookBub or equivalent as well as print book giveaways. I haven't personally attempted to calculate cost of acquisition, but in general, I think having a first book for free in a series and using ongoing marketing techniques keeps the cost down.

Score: 7. Indies use free and low-cost methods to attract customers on retailers where customers already shop.

(5) Cost of value delivery. How much does it cost to deliver this product?

Professional editing and cover design generally sits between $500 - $2,000 in total, and are recommended, although many indies do without them.

For ebooks, the delivery cost is taken out of the royalty at the 70% rate for Amazon, which is why you should be minimizing file size by removing images at that level. But in general, delivery rates for ebooks are low to non-existent. Publishing on the ebook stores directly is free, and the distributor takes a cut on sales.

For print books, print-on-demand delivery costs are billed to the customer as shipping, and the author receives the royalty from what's left, after the distributor's cut.

Score: 9. Very low delivery cost.

(6) Uniqueness of offer. How unique is your product in the market and can people copy you quickly?

Yes, every book is unique, but the product itself is not particularly unique. I will absolutely acknowledge that there are other action-adventure thrillers out there in the Dan Brown style niche, and my ARKANE novels fit in that grouping. Any of those books may satisfy a customer's desire for fast pace, global locations, religious conspiracy, and explosions, but only my books contain my spin on tales created from my own adventures. So for fiction, this question is hard to answer, and probably comes down to the author's voice and the customer's desire to hear your particular spin on the genre.

For non-fiction, it's a certainty that you can write similar books in a niche and customers will buy the books. Just look at how many diet books there are, or how many books on specific self-help topics.

Score: 5. Uniqueness based on the author's voice within a genre.

(7) Speed to market. How quickly can you create something to sell?

Speed to market is one of the most commonly cited reasons to self-publish, and indie authors certainly have an advantage over traditional publishing here. We can upload an ebook and it will be selling in 4-72 hours, depending on the site. We can get even print books up for sale within a couple of weeks. Traditional publishers have such long pipelines that many authors won't see their books hitting the shelves for six months to two years after they have completed the book.

But that's the publishing side. The creation of the book will take as long as it takes you to write, edit, and polish your manuscript to completion. That time will depend on what you're writing, whether it is in a new series, how much research you need, how experienced you are, and other variables. What I can say is that the more books you write, the better you become and, often, the faster you become, too.

Score: 10. With online technologies, speed to market as an indie is super-fast!

(8) Upfront investment. How much do you have to invest before you're ready to sell?

I've tried businesses that involve a lot of upfront investment. Try starting a luxury scuba diving charter boat business in New Zealand! Or property renovations for on-sell. Both of those require large investments upfront before anything is ready to sell and you can start to see some return. I made substantial losses on those businesses and gave up both of those ideas. (If you're interested, I go into a lot more detail in my book, *Career Change*.)

Authors have a very low startup cost, as the overheads are practically nothing with a book. You only need a computer and an internet connection. It's definitely recommended that you budget for a professional editor and a professional cover designer, but many indies still manage without, especially at the beginning. Publishing is free or very cheap if you know what you're doing! If you don't know what you're doing, check Appendix A: Resources for more on self-publishing.

Score: 8. Low startup costs and high profit potential with volume.

(9) Upsell potential. Are there related products that customers might also buy?

This is the power of the backlist, which many authors who have been writing for years are now realizing as they get their rights back. The backlist seems to be any book that is not the one in the current promotional cycle, but of course, with digital sales, there is no end to the promotional cycle. A book is always new to a new customer, even if it was written years ago. If you have ten books in a similar genre, or the same series, you absolutely have related products that a customer may buy and you can link to them in your back matter. You might also have boxsets containing more of your books for a better price, or other products like consulting and courses (mainly for non-fiction authors).

Score: 10. If you focus on writing more books in related niches, your backlist will grow and you can always upsell.

(10) Evergreen potential. Once the initial offer has been created, how much additional work will you have to put into it in order to keep on selling?

Books are fantastic products because they are scalable. You create them once and then you can sell them multiple times in multiple formats. Compare that to my old job as a business consultant, where I was paid once for every hour I worked. Work for time is not scalable and we will never make any more time. So scalability is one of the fundamentals of the book business model.

Scalability was one of the main reasons I moved into the online product creation space in 2008. But the penny only dropped for me on evergreen potential in early 2013 when I finally realized that fiction doesn't age, and that the stories you write today can keep selling for the rest of your life and after you die. Compare that to non-fiction, much of which does age and therefore has to be updated or removed over time. I love writing both, but it's the fiction that will likely last the longest, that is truly evergreen.

Score: 10 – for my thrillers.

Kaufman suggests that a score of under 50 means you should try another idea. I make my score 70, which means that being an indie author writing fiction reasonably fast in a popular genre is a decent business idea. Judging by the numbers at AuthorEarnings.com, we already knew that! But it's interesting to break it down.

Your turn! Evaluate your own business model using this framework and write down your scores for each area.

2.5 Contracts

This section is just an overview, but for more detail I highly recommend reading *Dealbreakers: Contract terms that writers should avoid* by Kristine Kathryn Rusch. It is just a few dollars for a book that could save you thousands and a lot of heartache. I consider it a must-read book if you are going to sign any publishing contracts. (Please, please, I'm begging you to read this book! I've had way too many horror emails and I don't want you to be the next one!) I also recommend *The Freelancer's Survival Guide*, also by Kristine Kathryn Rusch, which includes how to negotiate anything.

Please note: I'm not a lawyer and I'm not giving any legal or financial advice in this book. For any specific questions, please ask an intellectual property lawyer who specializes in publishing contracts.

Most of us have grown up with the assumption that the only legitimacy in writing a book is to be published by a 'known' publisher, to be chosen as something special by the gatekeepers. Having an agent and a publisher gives a writer status and prestige, and even with the indie revolution, many authors still feel the pull of the traditional deal.

If you want this, that's absolutely fine! It's your book and you're allowed to want whatever you want. You're allowed to sign contracts with agents and publishers, and, in fact, you should, if it best suits your book project. I'm not anti traditional publishing at all and have a couple of deals myself. It's all about what's right for the individual and each specific project.

But it's important to be aware that many authors have signed contracts because they were so keen for a deal that they didn't consider what they were signing. So, you need to be aware of the ramifications of any contracts that you negotiate and sign. You have to act as the CEO of your own business, and not sign anything that could hurt you later. You are responsible for anything you sign so you can't complain about it later if you didn't do your due diligence.

If you're at the beginning of your career and you're excited about the possibility of an agent, you might be tempted to sign anything. But please, think longer term about the possibilities of your writing future. Here are some of the important things to watch out for, but of course, you should talk to a professional for your specific contractual terms.

Agency contract

A few years back, I had two New York agencies interested in representing me and I went through the agency contracts in great detail. One of them included a clause where the agent would receive 15% of everything I published, regardless of whether they sold the work. I queried whether that included self-published work and they said yes, because they would build my author brand and so they would be responsible for my success. Considering how much work I have put into building my own brand, that raised a red flag, and when they wouldn't remove the clause, I happily went with the other agency who had a simple, fair contract with a clear clause that they would not be taking a share of self-published work. (I later split amicably with that agency, not an uncommon occurrence in publishing.)

Another important clause relates to the distribution of funds. I specifically stated that any payments should be split by the publisher and go to the agent at the same time as the author. Some agencies get the full royalty payment into their bank account and then distribute to the author later, which means you could be waiting a while for your money and the power differential in any future negotiation is tipped in the agent's favor.

Which rights does the contract include and which will the publisher actually exploit?

I have a friend who signed a World English contract for all formats (ebook, print, audiobook) but the publisher only put out print and ebook versions in one territory (Australia/New Zealand). That meant she couldn't self-publish or look for another publisher in the huge markets of the US and UK, as well as the rest of the world. She couldn't sell audiobook rights separately, even though the publisher had no intention of exploiting those rights. So, the rule to keep in mind is: Only sell the rights you want the publisher to have and that they intend to exploit, and specify the period in which they must do so, otherwise you get the rights back.

A recent contract of mine originally included audiobook rights alongside the ebook-only deal I had agreed to. I asked for that clause to be removed and it was, so now I can use ACX to try to get a German audiobook produced.

You also need to plan for success. There's a great section on film rights in *The Successful Novelist* by David Morrell, who wrote *First Blood*, which became the Rambo franchise. David pulls back the curtain on the realities of film and sequel rights as well as the all-important merchandising, which can be the author's best chance at making decent money off a film. Of course, 99.9% of us will never have a film deal, but if your contract has negated any chance of you sharing in the profits of that eventuality, you need to renegotiate that clause.

So, check very carefully what rights the contract includes and make sure that you really understand all the sub-rights.

How much you get paid for your rights

Authors get paid a royalty percentage depending on the type of book, how it sold, numbers sold and other factors that should be documented in your contract. This will likely be a complicated section in the contract so make sure you understand it.

Some contracts have escalator structures, so if you sell more books, you can get a higher percentage of royalties. This is particularly important with ebook sales, as indies know that we all make more money from ebooks. Do the sums on how many you think it's realistic that you'll be selling with a publisher, vs. how you might do on your own and then compare the percentage royalty and income you might expect.

Term of the contract and rights reversion clause

How long is the contract for? When can you get your rights back?

Remember how precious your rights are over the long term. Your publisher is not doing you a favor. They are not a charity. They want to make money from your book. But what if you're not happy with the way the book has been handled? What if you hate the title and the cover? What if the book sinks like a stone, the publisher doesn't do any marketing, and you know you can do better yourself? How long before you can do it your own way?

The contracts I've signed have included a specified number of years in the license period, and then with written notice,

I can get my rights back or the deal becomes non-exclusive. Most contracts will have an 'out of print' clause which, of course, with digital publishing and print on demand, means you may never get your rights back as the book will never be out of print.

Do not compete clause

This clause may stop you publishing during the term of the contract

- Under the same author name.

- In the same 'world'.

- With the same characters.

Think about that in more detail. For example, for a three-book deal, it may take three to five years to get those books out, in which time you're not allowed to publish anything else related to it, perhaps even under your own name. Unless you have a multi-six figure advance, it's unlikely that you can live on the money you get from this deal for long. Perhaps you want to write and sell other books in the same series, maybe self-publish a novella to keep your characters fresh in the reader's mind. Perhaps you want to write a new series under your same author name. This clause limits your freedom to do any of that, so be very wary of it.

How do you get out of your contract?

Your contract with a publisher or with an agent should include how to terminate the agreement. Of course, as with a marriage, you're hoping that everything will be rosy and wonderful for many years. But what if it isn't?

I 'broke up' with my first agent amicably and by mutual agreement. It's a common thing to happen, although not really talked about. The agency agreement I signed included the process for splitting up, so it was clear how it would happen. You need the same on your publishing contract, even if it is only for a specific number of years.

Many authors now get their rights back by negotiating with the agent or publisher they signed with. Check your contract and see an intellectual property lawyer if you're having issues.

2.6 Copyright and piracy

This chapter is just an overview, but for more detail I highly recommend reading *The Copyright Handbook*, by Stephen Fishman, which covers everything you need.

Please note: I'm not a lawyer and I'm not giving any legal or financial advice in this book. For any specific questions, please ask an intellectual property lawyer.

Questions about copyright and piracy are common when writers are just starting out. Many people are concerned about sending their work to an agent, or even an editor, in the fear that someone will steal their words.

In my experience, this fear lessens over time, as you realize that only the most famous people get heavily pirated, and by then you don't have to worry anyway! You also realize that ideas are nothing, execution is everything, and that obscurity is far more of a concern than piracy. Here's a little more detail on these topics.

Copyright

Copyright belongs to the writer and is granted as a protection for creators. It remains with the producer of the work and it is in the expression, not the idea. You can't copyright an idea or even a book title, in English at least. Authors can license the right to a work for a particular term (how long), and for a particular amount of return (how much), but the copyright remains with the author. In most of the world, the default length of copyright is the life of the author plus either 50 or 70 years. Any work that is no longer protected by copyright is said to be in the public domain. For example, Sherlock Holmes is now in the public domain.

Copyright is yours on creation of the work, and you don't need to register the work or mail your manuscript to yourself in order to prove it. You don't even need a copyright notice on the work anymore – that became optional in 1989, although most still use it. Copyright is a passive right, and the power lies in the fact it exists. You can't stop people infringing copyright, but it gives the holder the power to sue the infringer.

Many authors also have questions over possibly infringing other people's copyright through the use of images, quotations from text, song lyrics or other works. This is where the principle of 'fair use' should be examined on a case-by-case basis.

"An author is free to copy from a protected work for purposes such as criticism, news reporting, teaching, or research as long as the value of the copyrighted work is not diminished."

Stephen Fishman,
The Copyright Handbook

So using quotes from other books in your own work is usually fine, but there are issues with song lyrics, poems and images, as the whole piece or a greater proportion will be used. If in doubt, get written permission or just avoid using. If you do use a quote under fair use, always attribute the author.

Creative Commons licenses enable a standardized way to allow permission to use your creative work with specific conditions. They are a modification of copyright, ideal in the online world for sharing and remixing. For example, my photos on Flickr all have a Creative Commons license, specifying attribution, non-commercial. That means you're welcome to use them for whatever you like, as long as you cite my profile as the source and don't sell the images or use them commercially. So you could use them on your blog, for example, but you couldn't use them on a book cover. Most of the images I use on my own blog are Flickr Creative Commons images, and you will see the attribution at the bottom of the post. Author and digital activist Cory Doctorow shares some of his work under Creative Commons, and writing/reading app Wattpad also uses it.

For more on copyright, listen to this interview on rights - http://bit.ly/1tXqcdX - or read *The Copyright Handbook: What Every Writer Needs to Know* by Stephen Fishman.

Piracy

Yes, piracy happens. People may download your books and read them for free, especially if you are not releasing your books in a format people want. Some people may even try to resell your work themselves, although mostly only big names get hit with this level of piracy – the rest of us have a harder time getting our books into readers' hands!

So it's sensible to have some monitoring in place to watch out for piracy. You can monitor your web presence through Google Alerts, which will send you an email daily with any mentions of you on the web. Set up your name, your book names, your company name and anything else you want to monitor. You can also do regular searches on Amazon, and you may be contacted by them if they suspect anything untoward. For example, when my book, *One Day in Budapest*, was included in the *Deadly Dozen* boxset, I received an email from Amazon asking whether I was the copyright holder. If you have been pirated, you can contact the website host or the online distributor to rectify the situation.

But don't let the fear of piracy stop you from getting your creative work into the world! Here's why you shouldn't worry.

Most dedicated readers prefer to buy books rather than take stolen copies.

Your reading public are generally book lovers and voracious readers. Most people are also law-abiding citizens. Most are honest and want to compensate you. Trust your public. I have a personal example of this. I saw from my stats that one lady had bought two copies of the same ebook from my site. I emailed her, assuming that she must have clicked the button twice by mistake, and tried to refund her. She explained that she had bought a copy for herself and one for a friend. I was thrilled by this honesty!

Some authors are allowing piracy deliberately in order to promote book sales.

Paulo Coelho, author of many books including the worldwide hit *The Alchemist*, leaked his ebooks in Russia on piracy networks deliberately. His sales went from 1,000 to over 1 million per year. Coelho said, "Don't be fooled by the publishers who say that piracy costs authors money."

Piracy can be seen as marketing.

Many authors now give ebooks away for free and it is a recommended strategy to gain more readers for a print copy, or at least for a second book. Tim Ferriss launched The 4-Hour Chef on BitTorrent, deliberately releasing a section of the book onto the file sharing network, which drove sales back to Amazon. Neil Gaiman has also spoken about how piracy helped the sales of his books - http://bit.ly/1w34AfE

"Obscurity is a greater threat to authors than piracy"

This quote is from Tim O'Reilly, from O'Reilly Media and is absolutely true. It is better to be pirated and out there in public getting some eyeballs on your work than it is to have your unpirated, unseen manuscript sitting in a drawer where no one can find it or you.

Here is the word from JA Konrath, who also discusses piracy vs. obscurity and answers common questions on the subject - http://bit.ly/1plRfJm.

2.7 Production plan

"I do not over-intellectualize the production process.
I try to keep it simple: Tell the damned story."

Tom Clancy

I've worked in factory accounts departments, and walked the floors of production plants alongside whizzy robots and machines making things. The term production plan fills my mind with questions about which raw materials are needed for which batch of product, and how to work back from shipping dates to when each product needs to be made. That's one extreme, but many professional authors are now creating production plans for their own writing business.

You can't exploit the rights for your books unless you have books to exploit! If writing is your business, and you want to take it to the next level, you need to know what your production plan is. This will keep you accountable, and ensure you satisfy your customers on a regular basis. I consider this an advanced way of working, and 99% of authors don't have a production plan. But when I talk to the really successful indie authors, the big earners, they all have production plans, which is why I now have one, too!

It doesn't need to be anything too flash, just a one-pager with the next 12 months and which projects you'll work on and when. You can include this list in your business plan, covered later in Part 8. You might think this is too simple, but even just thinking ahead a few months will help. Calculating how long it will take to produce work and when you need editors and cover design, as well as factoring in breaks and 'real life' stuff, will help you to understand how many books you can write in a year and therefore how much income you can possibly make. It will help you with a longer-term focus for your business.

You can use a spreadsheet with months on, or just a Word document. I have a two-page document broken down into months and what should be happening per month. For example, in the month I am writing this I have:

- Research *Inquisition*, a full-length ARKANE thriller

- Finish first draft creative business book (this one!)

- Edits for *Delirium*, London Psychic Book 2

- Publish *Pentecost* print edition in German

I have similar one-liners per project that go out in a rolling 12 month period, plus some notes at the end for ideas for other books. I also have a list on the wall of books to write this year to keep me focused. You can take it down to number of words targeted and written. It's up to you.

My physical Filofax diary is also critical for time management, and I block out weeks for specific projects, including when I should be working in the London Library in order to spend focused time on production.

Here are some of the factors to consider in your production plan:

- **How many books do you want or need to write this year?** This will depend on your business model and how your cashflow works, as well as your speed and confidence in writing. Some authors put out a book every month or bi-monthly and money for those books (as a self-published author) starts to kick in two months later. Most authors see an increase or at least a spike on launching a new book, and it is generally found that the more books you have, the higher the income you will receive.

- **How long does it take you to write each type of book?** For example, it takes me six to nine months to get a new full-length fiction book out in an established series, two to three months for a novella, and around four months for a non-fiction book. I can work on some things concurrently, but I'm a reasonably slow writer compared to many. I also like to 'rest' my manuscript after first draft so that I forget it before editing and this adds at least a month to the schedule.

- **When do you need extra time in your plan?** For example, when are your kids on school holidays? Or when are you away?

- **How much advance notice do you need to give** your editor and cover designer? Put approximate dates in the diary so they know they can expect to receive work then. This accountability also helps you to deliver on time.

You should now be able to come up with a production plan, even if it is only basic. There are no rules, so start with a short list of projects and rough dates and make it more detailed over time.

Part 3: Employees, Suppliers and Contractors

3.1 Definition

This section explores the people who work for your business, whether they are directly employed (employees) or other professionals working on a contractual basis (suppliers and contractors). A professional author is never really a self-publisher, as the term implies that you do all the work by yourself – and that is never the case when you're professionally publishing and running a business. That's why I like the term independent author. I run my own independent business, but I choose to pay professionals to help me.

My current team consists of the following regular service providers:

- Fiction editor
- Fiction proofreader
- Non-fiction editor
- Non-fiction proofreader
- Book cover designer
- Interior book designer
- File formatter for complicated non-fiction books
- Graphic designer
- Podcast transcriptionist
- Virtual Assistant
- Technical help for my blog/website
- Bookkeeper
- Accountant

These are generally contractors who work per project, or per hour. I have other people – beta readers, accountability partners – who are not paid, but are an essential part of my process as well.

What roles do you need in your current business? Do you have people in place for each of these?

Employees are people who belong to the business for the longer term. Your business has an ongoing relationship with and responsibility to employees, as well as having to pay them as an ongoing concern. The legal and tax definition of an employee varies by country. For example, the HMRC in the UK has a checklist where someone is likely to be an employee if you can answer 'yes' to these questions:

- Do they have to do the work themselves?
- Can someone tell them at any time what to do, where to carry out the work or when and how to do it?
- Can they work a set amount of hours?
- Can someone move them from task to task?
- Are they paid by the hour, week or month?
- Can they get overtime pay or bonus pay?

Based on this list, it's unlikely that an author engaged in publishing purely their own books will have many, if any, employees. However, some authors move into setting up publishing companies or working with other authors, so they may employ people over the longer term.

Suppliers are people you pay to provide you with materials, products, or services. You may have an ongoing relationship with them, but payment is generally through deposits and invoicing at the end of a job. There may be a contract if the work is significant, or it just may be ad hoc. You request a product/service, it is delivered and then you pay and the transaction is over. There may also be monthly recurring payments, for example, for transcription or virtual assistant services.

3.2 You. The writer.

If you have set up a company, you are likely to be the first – and perhaps the only – employee, and it's important to consider the responsibilities that go along with this relationship. If you take this seriously, it will flow through into what you do every day.

Being a professional writer means treating it like a job and putting in the hours. Sure, sometimes it's amazing and brilliant and we're the luckiest people in the world because we work at something we love. But some days it's difficult. Writing a book is hard work, and no one promised that making a living as a writer would be easy. Taking your role as an employee seriously can help you with the discipline of showing up every day and doing the work. I heard thriller author Lee Child speak at Harrogate literary festival one year and he said that the job of being a writer is just like being a trucker. Don't make excuses about not feeling like it today. You just get in your truck and drive.

What do you promise to the company?

As the employee of a company, your main obligation is to spend a specific number of hours per week on specific tasks.

- Writing and producing products for the company to sell

- Publishing-related tasks

- Marketing and customer service tasks

- Up-skilling and learning more in order to improve your work

You also need to make sure that you manage your diary to balance personal commitments alongside your work.

What does the company promise to you?

In return for your work, the company usually promises certain things. For example,

- **Salary.** My company pays me a monthly salary as an employee.

- **Pension.** My company pays a pension for me as an employee. Although I don't believe that I will ever want to stop working, I do think that putting money aside for later in life is critical.

- **To pay the appropriate taxes** and file the legal paperwork for me as an employee.

- **To invest in my development** through a training budget for physical and online courses, conventions, and research trips for book projects.

- **To provide a working environment** that I can produce in, which includes a laptop, internet access and membership of the London Library.

Put your company hat on

Of course, your role as employee/writer is only one side of the equation. You also need to put your company hat on and think about the bigger picture. I'm also the Director of my company and I receive dividends as a shareholder, so it's also my responsibility to consider the longer-term prospects for my company, which means working on the business itself, not just in the business. This includes:

- Thinking about the strategy for the business.

- Making sure there is adequate cashflow to meet the responsibilities of payroll and pension for the employee.

- Planning for the longer-term future of the company and how to best position it for the next five to ten years.

- Making decisions about products, expenditure and time spent so that the company is in the best position.

This type of thinking can help you raise your head from the minutiae of writing and editing and look at the bigger picture. The mistake many small business owners make is to forget the 'working on the business' part, covered in detail in Part 7 and also in Michael Gerber's great book *The E-Myth*.

Write down what you promise to the company, what it promises you and how you will also work on, as well as in, your business.

3.3 Co-writing partners

The co-writing model is used by some big names in the industry to expand the number of books that they put out a year. James Patterson, Janet Evanovich and Clive Cussler use it, and you'll see the names of many other authors in smaller letters on their covers. There are also plenty of partnerships who work under one name. Nicci French, the British crime author, is actually a husband and wife team.

In the self-publishing world, Bob Mayer and Joe Konrath are now using the technique, as well as Jeremy Robinson with his Jack Sigler series. Indie romance mega-bestseller H.M. Ward has also moved to this model. Sean Platt has several co-writing businesses: Realm & Sands with Johnny B. Truant and Collective Inkwell with David Wright. In the UK, writing partners Mark Edwards and Louise Voss span the indie and traditional world with various publishing contracts. Personally, I would love to get to the point of co-writing but finding the right person to work with, as well as taming my own control freakery, is difficult!

If you want to write with someone else, there are several things to think about:

- **How will you approach working together?** Do you share ideas upfront? Does one person handle the outline and editing and the other write the first draft? Do you write alternate scenes? Who has final say on editing/cover design, etc? How will you split the marketing? These questions are probably the most important aspect of the whole arrangement. You need to know yourself well, and from interviewing people who co-write, the most important thing they say is to "leave the ego at the door." There's no place for ego in a co-writing relationship, it's truly a joint creative project and when the book is finished, it shouldn't be important who did what, as long as the effort is fairly split.

- **Contractuals and money.** How will you set up the contract for the split of the royalties? Who owns the copyright? If self-publishing, whose account will it be published from? Who will split the money and by when? Who has access to reporting?

- **Prepare for success as well as the potential of a split**. What happens if the book is optioned for a movie? What happens if you get offered a publishing deal for it? What happens if one person wants out of the agreement? What happens if one party dies? What happens if you end up hating each other? No one goes into a marriage expecting divorce, yet over 50% of partnerships do split up, so be very careful in setting your agreements up for co-writing.

Author collaboration

Co-writing is generally about creating new works together, but collaboration between authors of a similar genre is a step towards that. Digital publishing has enabled short-term projects that bring benefits for authors over a shorter period of time. Multi-author boxsets or simultaneous launches have become popular ways for authors to do joint promotion and get their work in front of a wider audience. Many authors also do joint launches and marketing activities in order to boost their profiles together. Promoting each other's books on email lists is also a great idea.

In my opinion, collaboration is one of the most powerful tools an author can use, so even if you're not ready for full-blown co-writing, consider networking with authors of a similar genre and looking for collaborative opportunities.

3.4 Editors

Editors are perhaps the most important supplier for your business, because they make your words sparkle. They are the polish you need on your work before you release it to the world.

You can and should edit your own work to the point where you just can't stand it anymore. Then it's advisable to give it to someone else. You can't see the words when you have lived so close to them, and editors will pick up so many things that you missed. A good editor is well worth the money, in my opinion.

Here are the different types of editors and why you might choose to use them. I have found that the terminology may change between countries and also between editors.

Structural editors / content editors

The job of the structural editor is to help you to shape the whole book into something readable, and their feedback is often in the form of a report or comments on the manuscript at a higher level. For fiction, they will look at plot, characters, setting, dialogue, theme, symbolism, and other factors that will impact your story. For non-fiction, it will be more about your message, the content of your chapters, what is missing, and how you can more effectively communicate with your readers.

I've had several structural edits for my fiction, and they have been invaluable in helping me understand what makes a good story. I recommend it particularly if it is your first book, when your learning curve is the steepest. You might think the book is finished, but it's likely that it isn't!

Line editors/ copy editors

This is the classic 'red ink' edit, where your manuscript should be ripped apart! Remember, you are paying someone to be critical, so if you just get a clean manuscript back with "good job!" on it, the editor is not earning their keep. This edit will be incredibly detailed, and you should have corrections, comments and suggestions all over it. It's a time-consuming job to do and so it will be the most expensive kind of edit. You'll generally have to book in advance as well as pay a deposit for the work.

You definitely want to use an editor who enjoys your genre, and many editors will be upfront about what kinds of book they will work on. You can get a couple of sample pages edited in order to 'interview' them. I've had several editors and consider it a bit like dating, in that you don't expect to find a partner for life on the first date.

Technical editors / fact checker / legal check

If you have a niche book that requires technical specialization, then you may want to find a technical editor to make sure everything is correct. If you have a non-fiction book that requires factual accuracy, then getting an external fact checker might also be advisable. Some authors may also hire someone to read for legal issues, if the topic is liable to be controversial.

Beta readers

These are people who enjoy your genre, and they can be paid or can also sometimes read for free. They might be general readers, or may be specialists. For example, I have an ex-coroner, Garry Rodgers, who beta reads my death scenes and comments specifically on matters related to corpses!

Provide questions for your beta readers, for example, where did you stop reading? What did you skip over? What did you really like? Was there anything you didn't understand? Were you left with any questions? This guides their responses. I usually have several beta readers, and if more than one person says the same thing, it definitely gets changed.

"Writing is rewriting"
– Michael Crichton

After each of these edits, you should expect to do another rewrite of your manuscript. The number of iterations of each will depend on your own process and the complications of the book.

For example, with my thriller *Delirium*, I actually 'lost the plot', finally understanding where that phrase comes from! I was so deep into the themes of madness that I had forgotten the plot and lost the characters, even after several major rewrites. I was also completely sick of the manuscript, and so my editor did a structural review along with line edits. Her suggestions on direction helped me to rewrite substantially as well as change the ending, and the book came together. Then she did a second line edit, and then it went on to beta readers and proofreading. I ended up rewriting five or six times.

Of course, you don't have to accept everything suggested by editors and beta readers. The aim is to improve the work, but you get to choose when to stick to your creative decision if it is important to you.

Proofreaders

Your manuscript should only go to the proofreader when it is 99.9% complete, and this is the final read before publication. It's good to have a fresh pair of eyes, someone who has never read the manuscript before. Their job is to find grammatical issues, typos and anything else that will impact the quality of the book. You should get back a manuscript with minor changes that you can update before publication. This is usually cheaper than any other kind of editing and personally, I have been grateful for every final proofread of my books! You might think the manuscript is perfect, but trust me, you can't see the errors at this stage of the project.

There's a Q&A with my fiction editor, Jen Blood, in Appendix F covering questions around how to find an editor and how to emotionally deal with the editing process. You can also find more about editing and a list of editors here: www.TheCreativePenn.com/editors

3.5 Agents and publishers

This is not a book on how to get an agent or a publisher. There are plenty of books on that, so I won't go into detail here. **This is more about how agents and publishers fit into your business.**

There's definitely a place for them, and many successful independent authors work with agents and publishers on different aspects of their business. It just depends on what is appropriate for each book project. For example, I'm an independent author, I had a New York agent for a time and I now have an agent for foreign rights only. I have a contract with a traditional publisher for the German version of *Desecration*. I have an audiobook contract with a small press in the US. I'm happy to sell foreign rights to publishers and work with agents on TV/film deals.

As CEO of your author business, it's important to remember that an agent works for you, not the other way around. The balance of power has been off kilter for so long in publishing, it's easy to forget that fact. Authors often pitch agents with an air of desperation and 'choose me' mentality, but think about it. Agents and publishers are not charities – they are not publishing your book out of the goodness of their hearts – they want to make money from it.

The agent usually gets 15% of your royalty income if they can sell the rights to your book. So you are paying them 15% for the life of the book, and if you don't sort out an end to the contract, it won't go out of print in this digital age, so that's the rest of your life and 70 years after you die. Some agency agreements even include a percentage of income from your self-published work, so read the contracts carefully and be aware of what you're signing.

In the same way, when you sign a publishing contract, the publisher will be getting a large chunk of your royalties. You may get an advance against these royalties but you will often only be getting 10-25% of the income from your book. The publisher will be taking the rest – so again, think about what you're giving away and whether you're happy to do that. The same is true with self-publishing but the figures are reversed – most of the retailers pay a 35-70% royalty to the author.

Some key things to think about:

- **Why do you want an agent?** Be honest. Is it just because this is what's expected? **Is your decision based on ego or business reasons?** If you do want an agent, what rights do you want to sell? There are different agents for different things, for example, I now have an agent for foreign rights only. There are some agents who will self-publish on your behalf, and others who will want to sell your domestic rights, others for movies and TV. You need to be very clear why you want an agent and what you're willing to give away. Try and keep the long view – will this still be a good deal in a year's time? In 10 years? In 30 years?

- **Before you sign anything, talk about the details around potential contracts.** Make it clear that there are some things you won't sign. Go back and review section 2.5 Contracts. It may be that this agent fundamentally disagrees with things you care about – in which case, you're better off without them.

- **Discuss how you will work together, including how to end the relationship**. Splitting up with an agent is a common practice, and most authors will have several in a career. When you're first starting out, this seems like crazy talk, but if you think of it like dating and a marriage, you'll see how human relationships naturally fade over time! Discuss how often you'll email and connect by phone/Skype and set expectations on both sides so there's a good balance. The agent will need time to work on submissions and won't want to be harassed by calls, but equally, you don't want silence for months on end. I had a lovely NYC agent and she was transparent in communication, connecting by email and Skype a few times a month. We agreed a timeline for sale and when that didn't come through, we split amicably with no hard feelings. In terms of your publishing contract, you need to understand how the contract will end and when, and how, you get your rights back.

- **When a contract is underway, make sure that any monies from the publisher are split at the source** and that your money arrives in your bank account at the same time as the agent's. Some agencies will take all the money and then distribute to the author later, so sort this out in advance to protect your cashflow.

3.6 Translators

The earlier chapter on rights covered various ways of getting the translation done, but if you decide to work with a translator directly instead of selling rights, this chapter should help.

It is a curious experience to see your book in another language, especially one you can't read and don't understand. The words are no longer your own, and there's a detachment that comes from this fact. But at the end of the day, it's your name on the cover and your brand that is represented, so you need to care about the quality of the work.

Translation is a creative endeavor and involves turning your work into another language, but also trying to communicate the nuance of the author's voice in a new way that works for this different audience. It is not a case of using Google Translate to change line by line. The book has to work as a whole, and the reader must not feel jolted out of their experience by jarring vocabulary. This means that the translator's work is skilled and they should be treated as a creative partner whose impact on the work is significant.

Working with translators

I've now worked with six translators for my books, and these are my recommendations:

- If you want to do joint ventures with royalty split, **decide which languages you want translated, and be clear on the business proposition**. For example, translating into Estonian because your grandparents live there is a personal reason for translation but is unlikely to result in sales. On the other hand, Spanish is the second most commonly spoken language in the world, with over 400 million speakers and a growing ebook market, so a royalty-split deal may pay off for both parties.

- **Interview the translators** you are considering. I use video Skype so that we can see each other. Ask them about their experience, and also why they are interested in translating this book. **Trust your instincts around whether you can work with this person.** If you're doing a royalty split, you could be involved with them for a number of years, so you need to be able to talk about things and get on in a professional manner.

- **Get a sample chapter translated** and ask native speakers to read and rate the samples. There are plenty of translators on Fiverr.com and PeoplePer-Hour.com who will translate a certain number of words for very little money. You can then choose based on the best feedback. The worst situation is to end up with a translation you can't publish, or that you publish and then gets bad reviews.

- **Agree a contract** that includes the terms for the book and the way you will work together. Many translators will have template contracts they usually work with and you can modify these, and you could also work with an intellectual property lawyer. Writer's organizations often have legal services that can help you check these contracts as well. At the end of the day, contracts are there to articulate the way you work and the terms of engagement, but they shouldn't be used to run the relationship. They are a last resort, so focus on honest and open communication to tackle any problems as they occur, rather than waiting until contractuals become an issue.

- Encourage the translator to **ask any questions** they have by email or via phone/Skype. There are always questions about what the author actually meant, and word choices will change based on intent. Being patient and helpful is the best approach.

- Be honest and open in your communication. I had Skype calls every couple of months during the translation process to ensure everything was on track and the translator was happy in their work. There have also been countless emails with questions and discussions, as well as discussing marketing tactics. This is basically a creative partnership endeavor, so you need to make time for it in your schedule.

Paying translators

There are a few ways to work with translators:

- **Pay upfront.** In this way, it is work-for-hire. It's recommended to pay in installments – a deposit upfront, a percentage halfway through the manuscript, when you could also get someone to proofread those chapters, and then on delivery. The final payment should only be made after you have checked the quality of the work with proofreaders or native speakers who like the genre.

- **Royalty split.** You agree a percentage royalty split and pay the translator for the length of time the book is published for. This means tracking sales and then paying what is owed on a regular basis. I set up a shared Google Drive spreadsheet which can be accessed by the translator, and I enter the sales by platform as well as the income amount after payment. I pay in the translator's currency by bank transfer/PayPal monthly after the money has been deposited in my account from the various publishing services. Again, this requires trust and honesty, and you will have to agree your own payment terms with your translator.

3.7 Book designers and formatters

Many authors seem to think that the design and formatting side of things is something only a traditional publisher can do for them. Or they think that it is so complicated that they had better leave that to their publisher or their agent, and 15% for the lifetime of the book is a fair exchange.

The truth is that you can get professional designers and formatters for print and ebooks, many of whom have worked for traditional publishing, for a decent price, or you can learn to do it yourself easily. There are several options for book cover design as well as interior formatting and design for both ebooks and print.

Do-it-yourself cover design

Unless you're a graphic designer, it can be dangerous to design your own book covers! Even if you're a graphic designer who does other things, there are still elements of book cover design that are particular to that type of product. However, there are some notable authors who design their covers and do incredibly well. For example, Bella Andre and Barbara Freethy, mega romance authors who have sold millions of books, both design their own covers. But in general, it's advisable not to DIY when people definitely do judge a book by its cover.

If you do want to design your own books, here are some resources:

- How to make your own book cover in MS Word – this tutorial goes into detail on how you can make a decent book cover yourself, including where to find images and how to use Word to create the cover: http://bit.ly/19NxtFP. You can also find templates and more help at DIYBookCovers.com.

- Use the Createspace cover creator tool if you want to use Amazon's Createspace for publishing - http://bit.ly/Y98J6J.

- Use Canva.com for Kindle covers.

Pay a professional for a cover

This is my preferred option, as my own attempts at covers generally look like a PowerPoint slide!

- I've gathered a list of Book Cover Designers here which I keep updated with new providers: www.TheCreativePenn.com/bookcoverdesign

- You can also keep an eye on The Book Designer's eBook Cover Design awards monthly, as you can find designers there for books you like.

- Check out the acknowledgments at the back of books to find the cover designer's details. Some authors also share information in the sidebar of their blogs.

Do-it-yourself interior formatting for ebooks

I know that some people don't want to mess around with ebook files. I used to feel like that too, but seriously, if you're intending to publish more than a couple of books, then try Scrivener. It will save you loads of money in formatting. You can output files in .mobi for Kindle and ePub for the other sites, as well as Word for your editor, PDF and other formats. It's most suitable for plain-text fiction and non-fiction.

If you're struggling with the functionality, I recommend the Learn Scrivener Fast training.

You can also use this free multi-part tutorial from Guido Henkel on formatting - http://bit.ly/1g0ibAM. Guido also has a great book on the topic: *Zen of Ebook Formatting*, so you can learn to do it yourself like a pro.

Professional formatting for ebooks

There are new services developing for ebook formatting all the time. Here are a few resources to start with, but googling ebook formatting and checking out the prices and testimonials will also help.

- Createspace conversion to Kindle file (for Amazon only): http://bit.ly/1plXblT

- Bookbaby formatting: http://bit.ly/1lwUym8

- Smashwords list of formatters: www.smashwords.com/list

- Polgarus Studios – I have used Jason for my own ebooks – www.polgarusstudio.com

- Guido Henkel, author of *Zen of Ebook Formatting*: http://bit.ly/1lwUym8

- EbookArchitects– for more complicated books: www.ebookarchitects.com

- EbookLaunch: http://bit.ly/1qxcmwv

Do-it-yourself interior formatting for print books

Formatting your print books yourself is a labor of love, and you have to be a detailed type of person to do it properly. I've done it myself before (a long time ago) and managed to get even the basic page numbering wrong, so now I hire people who enjoy that work and do it professionally.

But I do know some authors who format their own books, enjoy the process, and do an amazing job. If you want to format your book interior yourself, here are some resources:

- Createspace templates based on print book size: http://bit.ly/W73d2U

- Ingram Spark print template: http://bit.ly/1rL4knz

- Book design templates with all kinds of designs to choose from: http://bit.ly/1zWy95C

- Google tutorials for Adobe InDesign. There are lots of free videos and paid courses. You can also get the software in Creative Cloud on a monthly payment plan.

Professional formatting for print books

If you're like me and just don't find this kind of formatting fun, then you can hire a print book formatter for a reasonable price, or get this as part of a print-on-demand package.

- Createspace design packages: http://bit.ly/W74G91

- Lighthouse24: www.lighthouse24.com

- BookBaby interior design: http://bit.ly/1plZzJf

- JD Smith Design - my interior book designer: www.jdsmith-design.com

- Read *Choosing a Self-Publishing Service* by the Alliance of Independent Authors, which will give you the best advice about which companies to work with for your print book.

3.8 Audiobook narrators

The fast-growing audiobook market is now available to indies through ACX.com, which allows authors to work directly with audiobook narrators either on a work-for-hire basis or through royalty share deals. The work is on a project-by-project basis, but authors with series are likely to work with the same narrator multiple times if the business relationship works out.

How to find an audiobook narrator

ACX.com allows you to claim your book and then upload a sample for narrators to audition with. The platform is not available globally as yet, but give it time! You should include specific notes as to what you're looking for and you can pick a type of voice from the list. For example, the voice of an African-American male preacher in a thriller will be very different to that of a young woman in a coming-of-age story. The more information you give to your narrator in the notes, the better the fit will be. Once some auditions have been submitted, you can review them and pick the voice that fits your project the best.

However, in my experience, you won't have narrators rushing to work with you, especially if you're a new author with no platform! I found my ARKANE narrator, Veronica Giguere, by checking out the podcast fiction community and asking for recommendations, and asking directly. My London Psychic series narrator, Rosalind Ashford, found *Desecration* when she went looking for a darker book that required a female narrator, as she wanted a break from narrating romance. I do all my audiobooks on a royalty share basis, but many of the big-name indies pay upfront as work-for-hire in order to keep the larger chunk of income over time.

How to work with your narrator

Establish the timeline upfront and also make sure that you have allowed time to review the files. Things will get difficult if the whole book has been narrated and edited and then you decide the voice of your protagonist is somehow wrong. Make sure you discuss upfront any specific language issues, e.g. *Roger is from the north of England and Maria is Spanish, but neither should have a strong accent.* Give the narrator specific feedback with timestamps when you're quality checking the files, e.g. *At 18:24 minutes, Southwark is pronounced Sothuk, not South-wark.*

Be respectful of their skills and let some things go if they are not a big deal: for example, the word 'shone' is pronounced differently by British people vs. Americans. When I hear it read, it jars slightly, but I won't get that changed, as it fits with the rest of the narration and it's not a big deal. I only correct things when they are definitely wrong.

Remember, **this is a partnership and a creative process** – the narrator must be free to bring their interpretation to the project. You may also find yourself flinching at some passages, and this is your own fault! Make sure that you have re-read the book and that you're happy with the text before you start the narration process.

For more, check out these resources:

- Interview with Veronica Giguere: http://bit.ly/1oAGtPD

- Interview with Rosalind Ashford: http://bit.ly/1ugQkQd

- BOOK: *Making Tracks: A Writer's Guide to Audio-books and How to Produce Them* by J. Daniel Sawyer

- Interview with J Daniel Sawyer – how to record, produce and distribute audiobooks: http://bit.ly/1al2wHc

3.9 Bookkeeping and accounting

If you have a company structure, you will need to do accounts, but even if you are still at the beginning of your author journey, it is important to know what your income and expenditure is.

Your bookkeeper and accountant are an important part of your business team. There's more detail on financial reporting in Part 7, but this section goes into the people side.

Bookkeeper

Bookkeeping is the entry of income and expenses, invoices and receipts into a financial system, as well as checking bank statements, reconciling paperwork and doing the basic level of accounts. This should also give you reporting on your current position as well as profit and loss each month.

I tried to do bookkeeping myself for the first year of business, and it rapidly became a real headache for me. I hated doing it, so I put it off for months and resented the time I eventually spent doing it at year end. If you think about how much your time is worth on the creative aspects, you will realize that spending some money on a bookkeeper is a good use of funds.

I found mine on Gumtree.com and specified someone who could come to my flat once every couple of months for ad hoc work, so it would only suit someone who didn't need a regular income, or worked on multiple jobs. I interviewed a number of candidates and chose a lovely retired bookkeeper who still wanted some extra income. It's one of the best things that I could have done for my sanity and overall business happiness!

Accountant

Your accountant will look after the legal and tax obligations for your business, as well as the financial reporting. They may also advise you on how to optimize your financial situation. I generally only talk to my accountant when it comes time to prepare the yearly accounts and do all the statutory reporting necessary for my small business.

In finding a small business accountant, it's again good to ask for referrals from author friends. With online business, you don't need to have an accountant physically near you, although you will need one in your own country who specializes in your specific country requirements for tax and reporting.

If your income is significant, and you need investment advice, then you will likely have a financial advisor as well. Fingers crossed that we all need one soon!

3.10 Virtual or executive assistant

At some point, you may reach the stage when it would make sense to have an assistant take some of the workload from you, so you can focus on writing and connecting with your fans. That assistant can be someone local, but as an author's work is often online these days, a 'virtual' assistant (VA) can be the best option. However, the principles would still apply if you used a personal assistant actually in your home.

What does a virtual assistant do?

Here are some of the tasks you might consider outsourcing to one or more virtual assistants:

- Finding appropriate book reviewers and pitching for book reviews

- Transcribing podcasts or interviews

- Formatting newsletter/email blasts

- Formatting/scheduling blog posts and organizing guest posts

- Scheduling social media posting to multiple sites

- Book promotion scheduling and notification of free books

- Maintaining data on book files and testing them before upload

- Making images or SlideShares for books and creating other marketing material

- Posting serialized chunks onto Wattpad

- Updating sales figures into a spreadsheet or report

- Calculating royalties for co-authors/translators/ other business partners

- First-level research for books

- Pitching media or finding sources to pitch

- Setting up interviews

- Responding to email and screening emails

How do you find a virtual assistant?

Define your tasks exactly and the procedures for how to do them. This might include logins and guidelines for the tasks. I use Google Docs for this, as you can easily share the document with another person and update as you progress. You should also have some kind of idea as to how many hours a week this will be, for example, is it eight hours a week? Or eight hours spread over a month? Is it a specific project? Are there times when you want them to definitely be available or is the work flexible? Do you want specific providers per task or someone to play more of an executive organizational role?

Try personal recommendations first and use your social network to see if there are any candidates you already know in some way. You can also use a site like Odesk.com or PeoplePerHour.com or Bibliocrunch.com for posting jobs that people will pitch for.

Make sure you get references from happy clients, especially around confidentiality. Interview the candidates, either over email or Skype, and assess your compatibility and their skills. Agree on a trial period to see if it is working for both parties.

How much does a virtual assistant cost?

When considering the cost, you have to weigh up how valuable your time is and whether it can be spent on better things than some of the items outlined above. It's not about whether you CAN do it most of the time, it's about using your time strategically. I would suggest writing down the things only you can do e.g. the writing! Then write down everything else and assess what you are willing to pay for.

In terms of a ballpark figure, you can expect to pay anywhere between US$10 - US$50 per hour, depending on what the service is going to be. You'll need to get a quote from the individuals that you interview. Ad hoc services/projects can also be priced per task.

How do you work with a virtual assistant?

There is one overriding thing you must do: **Communicate!**

I have a rolling Google Docs worksheet with the tasks that I want doing, with a column for my comments and a column for my VA to note down things. We email every few days and Skype every couple of weeks. She also sends me To Do emails, e.g. when I need to send a book for review. As my VA is more executive level, I also ask for her opinions and suggestions on work.

Make sure that you have a timesheet along with the invoice and make sure you pay promptly. As small businesses ourselves, it's critical to respect the cashflow of other small businesses. You can pay by bank transfer but with the fees involved, PayPal may be the best option for all parties.

My own experience

I reached a breaking point towards the end of 2013, where my workload was higher than I could handle and I couldn't see a way to get it all done on my own. I tried using several virtual assistants and made a couple of mistakes:

- I didn't exactly define what I wanted from them or the desired end result

- I tried to get one person to do everything

- I didn't pay enough initially for a duplicate 'me' and was disappointed in the service I received

After learning my lessons, I changed my approach:

- **I eliminated tasks completely** if they weren't aligned to my strategic focus: for example, I stopped guest posts on TheCreativePenn.com and stopped following 400+ blogs in order to schedule on social media. This elimination, not delegation, approach was sparked by this interview with Charlie Gilkey from Productive Flourishing (audio, video and transcript available): http://bit.ly/1w3gk1A.

- **I split tasks into different groups**, so I have one person for transcription of my podcasts, another executive VA for high-level research and 'duplicate me' tasks, and I use PeoplePerHour.com or Fiverr.com for specific, measurable short-term activities.

A fantastic book to read on this topic is *Virtual Freedom: How to work with virtual staff to buy more time, become more productive and build your dream business* by Chris Ducker. This book will save you a lot of time and money if you want to get into using virtual assistants.

3.11 Managing your team

If you have an aggressive production plan with lots of product cycles going on at once and a diverse team, you might have a need for management tools to keep everyone in sync.

Here are some options for project management tools.

Google Drive

This is a free suite of tools that anyone can use. Here's how I use it for organizing my work:

- Google Doc for keeping a list of my upcoming podcast interviews, shared with my transcriptionist so she can plan her workload

- Google Doc for a running schedule of my blog posts and podcast interviews so I can plan when I need to schedule ahead

- Google Doc shared with my Virtual Assistant with a running list of activities for her to work on: we can both add notes so we know where we are with everything

- Google spreadsheet as a timesheet shared with my Virtual Assistant so we both know the hours she works, plus when she invoices and when I pay

- Google Doc shared with each translator with a work plan and dates so we both know who is working on what, as well as a spreadsheet for sales

I combine these tools with Things, a Mac app for desktop and iPhone which tracks all my To Do items with dates.

I also use regular email with my various team members, keeping them updated, e.g. telling my editor if the book will be a few days early or late. Plus I have Skype calls to go into more detail, which has been especially important for my translators as well as my Virtual Assistant.

Need something more substantial?

You can also try Asana.com or Basecamp.com, which are both extensive project management systems where you can assign tasks to people and manage email within the system so nothing is lost. It has reminders and follow-ups so you can keep everyone on track. This is too much for my own business right now, but Sean Platt, Johnny B. Truant and David Wright from the Self-Publishing Podcast use it for their multi-genre publishing empire.

Part 4: Customers

4.1 Definition

A customer is someone who pays you for a product or service. As authors, our ultimate customers are readers, people who consume our content. They may pay through a distributor, but ultimately, we have to please our customers in order to sell.

It's also important to remember that you're not writing just one book. This is a lifetime business.

You don't just want someone to buy a single book. You want that customer to love your book so much that they will buy everything you'll ever write. This is switching the mindset from the launch spike of one book to the lifetime value of the customer over the long term.

"The purpose of a customer isn't to get a sale. The purpose of a sale is to get a customer."

Bill Glazer, marketing strategist

4.2 Who are your customers?

This is one of the hardest things for authors to work out, especially at the beginning of the journey when very little has been written. Here are some further questions to help you work it out, as well as my own examples, which may help you with your answers. Ultimately, you will refine this over time as you write more and your voice develops.

Know yourself

We are often our own target market!

Start by writing down aspects of yourself that are revealed in your books that might connect you to people who would like to read your work.

I write non-fiction in order to understand what I think on a topic, and use the research process to learn more myself. This book was written to help me to streamline my own business, and my first book, *Career Change*, helped me to change career. When I think about non-fiction books I want to write, they are aimed at people like me, so I know the problems my customers have. They are my problems too.

I write fiction to explore themes that interest me around places that fascinate and characters that I would like to read about. I write fast-paced thrillers because they are what I love to read. This stems from my own background. When I hated my job, I wanted to escape it, so I would read on my commute and every coffee break and lunch time. Any book that took me away from reality was on the list!

Ultimately, we write what we want to read.

Since writing my darker fiction, I will say to a group that I am a taphophile – someone who likes graveyards. They make me feel peaceful, and I like to take photos or write there. When I say that, some people will think I'm weird, but people who understand will feel a connection and will likely check out my novels. There are other things, which inspire my stories: art and architecture, psychology, eso-terica, old manuscripts, religious relics, demons, myth and legend, apocalypse, and interesting locations. People who like the things that I do may turn out to like the books that I write.

What are you interested in? What are your passions? What do you like learning about?

For non-fiction specifically

What are the problems that your book is trying to solve?

What are the questions that you are trying to answer?

People generally buy non-fiction because they want to learn more about something or solve a problem. They may also buy because they trust the author, or follow their blog/podcast/platform.

This book is answering my own question – how do I go from being an author to running a business as an author? It's a question many have in an entrepreneurial age where the old rules are eroded and we have to navigate our own path as small businesses. In figuring out my own response, the aim is to help you, too.

What are the themes and characteristics of your book? (Fiction)

Figuring out the themes and characteristics of your book will help you decide who might like your book. What are the main aspects of the characters? What topics are covered? What can readers learn about? What places are featured? What themes crop up in all your work?

For example, my books *Desecration* and *Delirium* feature a psychic, Blake Daniel, who can read the emotions and history of objects, experiencing visions from the past. This allows him to help solve crime alongside Detective Jamie Brooke. So these books clearly have a supernatural side which will appeal to some, and also have a murder mystery at the heart. They feature the history of medicine, and the history of mental health, so people interested in those topics may also like them. All my books have a particular sense of place, as travel is so important to me, as well as independent characters, a strong sense of right and wrong, and a religious/supernatural or spiritual angle.

Write down the aspects of your book in this kind of list.

What are some similar books to yours? Who are the similar authors?

As a writer, you should also be reading widely in your genre. You probably read the books you want to write already, so you should be able to answer these questions off the top of your head, or at least by reviewing your bookshelf. You're allowed to have models for your writing, and in fact, when starting out, it's a good idea to have some role models from books, TV or movies to follow to get you started.

I started writing my ARKANE series with James Rollins' Sigma books in mind. I wanted to create an organization that allowed different characters to travel the world solving mysteries and getting into trouble on the way. Dr Morgan Sierra is also my alter ego! With my Masters in Theology, I wanted to revisit the aspects of religion that fascinate me, so I brought aspects of Dan Brown to the books. I also like the kickass action of Matthew Reilly, as well as Angelina Jolie in *SALT*, *Mr & Mrs Smith* and the *Tomb Raider* movies.

Desecration was described by one reader as "the love child of Stephen King and PD James," a combination of horror/ thriller and crime. My biggest influence is John Connolly's Charlie Parker series, which has a detective who works on the edge of the supernatural. When talking to people about my books, I can mention any of these names, and if the person recognizes the author, or reads those books already, they may like my books. If they look blank, it may be that they're not my kind of reader.

What category/ genre does your book fit into?

You need to know where to put your book on the virtual bookshelf, as that is where your customers search. If you try to switch your head from author to reader dispassion- ately, this will help! You might not like being put in a box, but there are rules that govern genres. You will likely fit into more than one category, but you need to think about where your customers might shop, so think broadly about the main features of your book.

Is there a detective in it? It might fit into crime.

Do the main characters end up together (happily) at the end? It might be romance.

Are there trolls/elves/other fantastical creatures? It's likely to be fantasy.

Is it set in space/the future? It might be sci-fi.

Is it a personal story that doesn't fit anywhere else? Perhaps it's literary fiction.

There are sub-categories within all of these, so spend some time browsing on the Amazon store and decide which are the most appropriate for your book.

Who are your customers and what do they want?

You can now turn your answers into an overview of what your customers are looking for, or a kind of customer profile. Here are mine.

My non-fiction customers – for Joanna Penn books:

- Are authors/writers who want to sell more books and become more successful

- Take their career seriously and want to learn and improve

- Are comfortable online

- Read books on writing, story, book marketing, and other things related to being an author

My fiction customers – for J.F.Penn books:

- Want escape into a fast-paced story

- Like an aspect of the supernatural/spiritual or religious in their books

- Are interested in global locations

- Like to learn something as well as get lost in a good story

- Appreciate independent female characters

- Read thrillers, crime, action-adventure, dark fantasy, some horror

Notice I'm not a fan of demographics, e.g. single women aged 25-40 who live in New York. I'm more interested in interests that span age groups, location and gender. I get emails from readers all over the world, from men and women, from priests and agnostics, from people in their teens to people in their 80s. But these readers fit into the same type of interest groups. In Part 6: Marketing, you will take this list and work out where these people might hang out so that you can target them specifically.

Write profiles for your customers. Split them into different sub-groups if you have multiple series or brands.

4.3 Customer service

Customer service for authors may be an unusual concept! But if you keep in mind that you have a lifetime in which to write, then ideally, once you have a fan, you want to keep them long term. Keeping customers happy is what customer service is all about, and pleasing readers will always help your business bottom line.

Write books for your customers

Earlier in this section, you identified what your customers are like and what they want. If you want to be of service to them, then you will write books for that customer base. This is the essence of the author brand, and writing books to satisfy your customers is the best way to grow your business.

Of course, you have to balance this with your own creative freedom, and you get to choose what you do with your time, but the most successful authors will say that writing to their audience helped them grow. I've also heard from two veteran writers, Bob Mayer and Colin Falconer, with 100+ books between them, that it was a mistake to diversify into multiple genres over their career, and that they should have narrowed their focus in order to penetrate a genre more effectively.

Connect to customers by having a list signup and by responding to email and social media

Email is still the most personal way to connect with people, and although the biggest authors are swamped and don't generally respond to everything, most of us are not. We have time to respond, or we can make the time, although of course sometimes it's difficult.

I love to ask people to hit reply and talk to me when I send out my email newsletter. I usually get some lovely responses and then we can have a conversation. Emailing your list should not be a chore! It's about connecting with your customers, sharing useful, entertaining or inspirational information, and also occasionally rewarding your customer base.

I'll admit to having 'impostor syndrome' as much as anyone – you know, that feeling that you're a fraud somehow, that this fan mail saying that someone loved your book isn't deserved. But you need to get used to receiving and responding to email from fans. I often print out lovely emails and stick them in my journal, which helps to combat 'impostor syndrome,' and to offset the (very occasional) nasty email I receive.

Reward your customers

You can include free giveaways, review copies, gift vouchers and other swag in your newsletter. You want customers to be delighted to receive an email from you, and ready to buy your next book.

Don't be an idiot

If you get bad reviews, if you get horrid emails, if you get haters on social media, if you get angry and frustrated, go cry in your room, or go punch a bag at the gym. Don't get online and vent. Don't pollute the air for the fans who love you. Don't give out negative energy. It only attracts more. Word gets around on social media and if you behave like an idiot, you risk losing it all.

If you go to conventions and people want a piece of you, smile and be nice, even if you're really tired and want to go back to your room. If you get thousands of people wanting you to sign books, sit and sign. Block out time for your fans and then try to be gracious and giving. Each customer is worth a lot to you over the long term. After all, we wouldn't be able to do this without fans to buy our work, and no sale is guaranteed.

Part 5:
Sales and
Distribution

5.1 Definition

A **sale** is the transaction between you and the customer for your product at a specified price. It's the point when the product actually changes hands. Many indies give away a lot of free books, but I'm taking that as marketing rather than sales, covered in Part 6.

Distribution channels are how your product gets to the customer, for example, an audiobook downloaded through iTunes. Distributors are the companies who facilitate the distribution, for example, Amazon facilitates the distribution of ebooks to Kindle customers. A major part of traditional publishing is print distribution, as they still control bookstores, airport retail and major outlets like Walmart or WHSmith. Handselling your book at a local fair is a distribution channel, as is an established speaking business where you sell at the back of the room.

5.2 Selling through distributors

There are a number of distribution options for our books. This is not a 'how to self-publish' book, so if you're unsure what each of these are and how to use them, please read, *Choosing a Self-Publishing Service* by the Alliance of Independent Authors, and/or *Let's Get Digital* by David Gaughran.

Physical bookstores, large retail outlets, airports, libraries, etc

You will generally need a traditional publisher to reach these types of outlets, but things are gradually changing as the attitude to indie books shifts. Ingram Spark is offering global distribution of print books to chain stores, independent bookstores, libraries, schools and universities, and more, so definitely check them out if print is a big part of your business model. Just make sure you check all the costs involved and factor in discounts and returns, which will impact your overall profit significantly. Do the figures before you commit, otherwise, stick with print on demand.

If you are serious about pursuing these outlets, read *Opening up to Indie Authors: A Guide for Bookstores, Libraries, Reviewers, Literary Event Organizers and Self-Publishing Writers* by Debbie Young, Dan Holloway and Orna Ross. This has a whole section for authors on how to approach and get your book into libraries and bookstores particularly.

Direct to eBook retail stores

The biggest ebook retailers now have direct self-publishing services that are available for free to encourage creators to distribute to customers directly.

The most popular services are:

- Amazon KDP for Kindle: kdp.amazon.com

- Kobo Writing Life: www.kobo.com/writinglife

- Nookpress for Barnes & Noble Nook: www.nookpress.com

- iTunes Connect for iBooks: http://itunesconnect.apple.com

- Google Play: http://bit.ly/1A2289D

The distribution method is through e-reading devices, mobile apps and online stores that each of these services provide. There are some exclusive services if you only use Amazon – KDP Select and Kindle Unlimited subscription service – so you will have to decide whether you want to use just those or distribute more widely.

eBook distributors

There are a number of companies that operate as distributors to a raft of ebook stores including the above, as well as subscription services like Scribd. These are the main ones offering free publishing with a percentage of sales to cover their service.

- Smashwords: www.smashwords.com

- BookBaby: www.bookbaby.com

- Draft2Digital: www.draft2digital.com

There are many other options but in general, you can evaluate any business based on how they make their money. Does the company make money when the author actually sells books? Or do they make money from charging the author before any book sales?

In general, it's recommended to use services that are free to publish on and just take a percentage of sales, as they are invested in your book sales success.

Print distributors

The main print book distributors for indie authors are:

- Createspace: www.createspace.com

- Ingram Spark (which uses Lightning Source and is aimed at self-publishers): www1.ingramspark.com

- Blurb: www.blurb.com

There are also a lot of other companies offering this kind of print and ebook distribution service. To save yourself time, money and heartache, read *Choosing a Self-Publishing Service* by the Alliance of Independent Authors in order to avoid the scams.

Audiobook distributors

Currently, there is only one audiobook company that makes it extremely easy for independent authors to exploit their audio rights, and that's ACX.com.

As the rights holder, you can load your manuscript to ACX and have narrators audition to read your books. You can also record the book yourself, but it must be done to exacting standards. You can then choose to do a royalty-split deal or pay the narrator in entirety for the book. You can also choose to be exclusive to ACX and Audible, which means that the book will also be available on Amazon, Audible, and iTunes. All of these decisions will impact your royalty percentage.

5.3 Selling direct

An important consideration for your business is diversity of income streams.

You don't want to be over-dependent on one source for your money, because if it dries up, you will suffer immediately and your business may fail. You will end up with no power in that relationship, and no choice but to do what that company wants in order to continue working with them.

The Amazon/Hachette dispute has been the catalyst for my own move into direct sales of books, even though I have been selling courses online for a number of years now. Amazon represents 60% of Hachette's ebook sales in the US, and 78% in the UK, according to GoodeReader in June 2014. Once another platform has that much control over your business, negotiations are always going to be difficult.

Where do you receive your revenue from?

How many different sources?

Is your business sustainable if that channel disappears or changes terms?

Indie authors love Amazon, because they pioneered self-publishing for ebooks and enabled authors to make a living online. But we're also aware of our dependency, and Amazon is a business, not a charity.

Jeff Bezos himself, in an interview on Charlie Rose, said that one day Amazon will be disrupted. It's their business, so they get to change the rules when they want. So do Kobo, Nook, Apple and any other companies that sit between the author and the customer. I'm not talking about exclusivity here – I publish on all these platforms and plan to continue doing so, but I can still build my own channel on the side.

Building a direct channel for sales is one option to grow an income stream that has no intermediary except a buy button. It also enables the author to learn more about their customers and create a direct relationship. Some customers are now actively looking to buy directly from artists, wanting to support creativity on the granular level rather than through a global conglomerate. I've had emails from people who refuse to buy from the big stores for ethical reasons, and the rise of indie movements in craft and farmer's markets as well as startup culture have made consumers more aware of the little guys and more ready to support them.

Here are your options for direct sales.

Sell ebooks/audiobooks/courses or other digital files from your website

Customers can manually transfer digital files onto e-reader or mobile devices in order to read them. This means that you can sell .mobi files for Kindle and .ePub files for other devices, as well as PDF or any other formatted files directly from your site, and use a shopping cart through PayPal or other services to process the payments. Customers can purchase directly on your site and download their product, and you receive the money shortly after. There are a number of services you can use.

I've been using e-Junkie.com for a number of years, and the $10 fixed monthly payment/no transaction fee as well as affiliate options are great for selling online. However, the customer's experience is not that intuitive.

You can also just use a PayPal Buy button on your site, but again, it's not very sophisticated and nowadays, there are options that include email and social integration, as well as analytics. When I decided to sell my books directly from my website, I evaluated the following options:

Gumroad

- Great customer interface. Supports creators in 40 countries. It's quick to integrate Gumroad onto your website, sell on Twitter, Facebook, YouTube, Sound-Cloud, and through your own email newsletter. You can set up discount codes. Detailed analytics.

- 5% + 25¢ per transaction with no additional monthly, hosting, or setup fees. Everything is covered: File hosting, file downloads, payment processing, payout deposits, customer support, analytics and dispute fees. Consideration for sales tax, including US rules.

- Specifically doesn't accept PayPal – explained in detail here: http://bit.ly/1rg0jVH - it's about control of the interface and customer experience.

- Can be used for physical items as well as digital. Includes subscription content - great for serials, or for recurring delivery of content.

- Used by Jim Kukral for his Go Direct book (all about direct sales!)

Payhip

- Everything you need to promote and sell your ebooks to your social network. Specifically aimed at being easily shareable. Customizable sales page, which is already attractive with the default options. Ebooks only.

- Pay what you want pricing + discount coupons. PayPal only payment. You are paid directly after purchase. Charges 5% per transaction, taken after PayPal fees.

- Google analytics integration.

- Used by Chuck Wendig on his book pages.

Selz

- Fantastically easy to set up and great design with a pop up within your website so the customer doesn't leave.

- 5% + 25c per transaction. Can use both credit cards AND PayPal.

- Easy social integration, as well as integration with Aweber mailing list. Responsive design means ability to buy on mobile devices.

- Audio and video previews.

- Can be used for physical, digital and services.

- Used by CJ Lyons on her book pages.

You should investigate all these as well as any other more recent developments in order to find what fits your business the best.

Personally, I am now using Selz for my ebook and audiobook sales direct from my website. You can see examples on TheCreativePenn.com/Store and also JFPenn.com/Store which both link through to individual product pages. My main reason was that, as a customer, I like to be able to pay by PayPal or bank card, so I wanted both options. I also like the audio and video extras in Selz, as I think multimedia will become ever more crucial in sales. It also integrates with my Aweber email lists so I can develop a list of buying customers, separate to the list of people who download my free stuff.

Sell print books/physical product from your website/online

Many authors buy and hold their own stock so that they can sell signed copies of books from their websites. Other authors have DVDs, physical products like T-shirts or other merchandise. Again, you can use PayPal Buy buttons on your site for physical sales as well, but for extended functionality, check out:

- Gumroad, Selz, e-Junkie all have physical sales options

- Woocommerce has specific WordPress themes and customization for physical products and catalogues

- Shopify

I don't do physical sales, so I can't share my experience. If you're going to go ahead with physical sales, please do your research and consider print on demand or drop-shipping, where the product is made and delivered straight to the customer without you having to hold stock. Otherwise, you will need to pay for stock upfront, hold it or warehouse it, as well as deal with shipping. Lines at the post office are no fun, and neither is a pile of unsold stock in your house. Trust me, I've made that mistake and made a business decision to focus on digital products primarily because of it.

Sell physical products in person

The rise of the indie movement across many industries has seen a renaissance in craft fairs, local markets, and people interested in buying directly from the creator. You may also be a public speaker wanting to sell books at the back of the room, or have some other existing physical distribution channel.

In the past, you needed to register for expensive swipe machines at banks in order to process credit/debit card payments in person as a small business. But there are technologies emerging now to suit the small business. These are mainly available in the US and Canada right now, but are spreading globally. Here are some examples:

- Square – a small plugin card reader for your phone or iPad. Accepts all major credit cards. Deposits next day into your bank account. 2.75% charge per swipe.

- PayPal Here – a separate card reader that works with your mobile. Charges a one-off fee for the reader and then 2.75% for chip and pin cards or PayPal.

- Intuit's Go Payment – Plugin swipe device with signature that works with your Apple or Android mobile and all major credit cards. Works with QuickBooks accounting software. Has pay-as-you-go or monthly rate charging with swipe rates of 1.75% - 2.40%.

- Amazon Local Register – Card readers and app. Charges 1.75% per swipe. Income can be used on Amazon or deposited direct to your bank account.

Asking your customers for support

There are also a couple of other models that come under the 'sell direct' umbrella.

- **Crowdfunding**. Sites like Kickstarter, IndieGoGo, or PubSlush for books allow fans to contribute to costs upfront so that special projects can be developed. It generally works best for original ideas, rather than asking for readers to pay for editing a book by a first-time author.

- **Patronage or support**. Amanda Palmer's TED talk on 'the art of asking' as well as her incredible Kickstarter campaign encouraged people to think more widely about how creative work can be funded. If you produce great work and your readers want your books, then they want to pay you for your time and your work. Patreon is a site that allows subscription payments to continue as long as the artist continues to produce work, e.g. $5 per comic produced. Some podcasters are now asking for 'support' of their work through purchase of books, products or by giving money directly.

All of these require an author platform

If you want to sell directly, or if you want to explore crowd-funding or patronage, you will need an author platform and people who know who you are and are keen to buy. You will need traffic to your website, and you need an email list so that you can tell people when there are books ready to buy. This all means that these options are for the more developed business, although it's good to start thinking about what you might want to do later.

5.4 Publishing imprint and ISBNs

Large publishing companies have imprints that specialize in certain genres of book. They also use International Standard Book Numbers (ISBNs) to track the various formats for each product. Many professional indie authors now emulate this setup, although it must be noted that you don't need to do either in order to sell your work online.

Imprint vs. setting up a company

Your legal company name, if you have set one up, does not need to be the name of the publisher that you use when you publish your work, or the author name that you use. There are different fields for each when you self-publish, so you can choose what you use. For example:

- Legal company name for tax records and banking – Pro Indies Limited

- Publisher name (imprint) – Summer Rain Romance

- Author name – Jemima Frances

- So you can use different names in each if you like.

Many authors are now using a publisher name that isn't their own name, as that might be considered more professional. A few years ago, bookstores would not have considered stocking self-published books, so many used an imprint name in order to appear as a micro-publisher. I think that attitude is changing but it's still a professional way to present your company and is an obvious choice for author collectives.

I use my legal company, The Creative Penn Limited, as my publisher on my print copyright page and I don't enter a separate publisher name when I publish on the ebook platforms. Yes, the company name contains my name, but as my primary business focus is digital, and I don't believe most ebook readers shop by publisher name, I don't think it matters. As with many aspects of running your own business, you have a choice and you get to make your own decisions.

ISBNs

ISBNs were set up in the 1970s as stock-keeping identifiers. Author names and book titles can be similar, so duplication issues were solved by these unique identifiers, which also worked well with computer systems emerging at the time. There are different ISBNs for the different formats of one book – so you might have one for paperback, one for ebook, one for audiobook, and one for a limited edition hardback. When you purchase the ISBN (they are free in some countries), you can enter specific data to be associated with it, such as your publisher name and information about the book.

Indie authors are divided on ISBNs, and whether you purchase your own depends on your business focus and whether they're free in your country. If you want your print book to be available in physical bookstores, then you should definitely get your own ISBNs and investigate options to produce and distribute the books. If ISBNs are free in your country, then go ahead and use them – why not!

If your focus is primarily online sales, you can actually publish everywhere without an ISBN if you go direct.

Although I started off purchasing my own ISBNs, I stopped using them a few years ago, because I couldn't see any evidence that having an ISBN actually made me more money.

In the UK, they cost £318 for 100 numbers (around US$540) or £846 (around US$1440) for 1000 numbers. Because I personally couldn't see the value, I publish direct to Amazon, Apple, Kobo and Nook, as well as using Createspace (which has free ISBNs) and ACX for audio, without using my own ISBNs. But let me stress again, I don't aim to get my print books in bookstores, so it works for my business model, but may not work for yours.

You can find out more about ISBNs by checking the site for your specific country:

- US Bowker - 10 for US$295

- UK Nielsen - 10 for £132

- Australia Thorpe Bowker - 10 for AU$84

- Canada CISS – Free!

- Or google 'ISBN + your country'

You will generally need to fill in forms and register as a publisher in order to get the numbers assigned.

5.5 Pricing

Pricing is one of the perennial topics discussed by authors and the publishing industry at length in blog posts and at conventions. Here are some things to think about.

As an indie, you choose the price and you can change it when you like

Self-published authors have a great advantage with price. We can change our prices when we like, testing various price points. Whatever you initially decide, you will likely change it later anyway. For example, you may start a book at 99c to get some initial readers and later, put the price up to $4.99 as your prominence grows. Or, you may start at $9.99 because you're sure the book will sell at that price. If it doesn't, drop the price and see what happens. There are no rules!

Of course, this pretty much only applies to ebook pricing, as there is no production and delivery cost for the book. For print books, your price is determined by the cost to produce and distribute plus your profit margin.

Pricing is a marketing technique

I had a consulting client once who came to me asking why his first book wasn't selling any copies. He had a great cover, a good title and an enticing sales description, but the ebook price was set at US$12.99. As a first-time author with no audience and no platform, there was no one waiting to buy his book. If you're a brand new legal thriller writer and the latest John Grisham ebook is $4.99, do you think people will buy your book at $9.99 instead? If you're writing non-fiction and the latest Malcolm Gladwell is at $8.99, can you charge $13.00 for something similar? Yes, you can. But will it sell?

One popular marketing tactic is putting your book on sale and advertising that new price for a limited time. This is the driving force behind the popular site, BookBub.com, which many authors use to spike sales for a short time based on the site's extensive email marketing.

Pricing is your decision, but put yourself in the customer's shoes

Who are the potential readers of your book?

Are they like me? I'm a high-volume reader, buying and consuming several books a week. We don't have a TV, so my main form of entertainment is reading. I read across many genres, but primarily thrillers, literary fiction and horror/supernatural as well as non-fiction entrepreneurship, psychology, and travel. I'm one of those whose reading has more than tripled since switching to digital a few years back, and whose addiction to One-Click payment expands the credit card bill monthly! But hey, books don't count as an expense, right?

My excessive reading makes me price sensitive, because I have a certain amount of money to spend on books and if they were all over $10, my reading would be severely curtailed! I also have certain expectations: I will pay more for an author I know and love and often pre-order those. I will pay more for a non-fiction book that gives me actionable advice. I shop by browsing categories I like and sometimes check the Daily Deal and BookBub for deals, making spur-of-the-moment buying decisions when pricing is low. The way in which I behave as a reader shapes my own pricing mechanisms.

The more books you have available, the more you can play with pricing

When you only have one book, stop worrying about pricing and just write another book. It's easy to get obsessed about it, but to be honest, you can't do much with one product. Once you have a few out, you can start to play with pricing. For example, in my ARKANE series, the first book *Pentecost*, is free and the other full-length novels are at $4.99, with the novellas at $2.99. I also have a boxset for $6.99, which is three full-length books at a discount, and a megapack of 5 books.

Using free

Free books can be a gateway drug to your work, enticing new readers into your world. They are a discoverability tool that many authors swear by, as they are out there being downloaded every day. They can be a great way to grow an email list as well as get reviews on a book.

Some people say that free books are devaluing your work, but you have to think about your body of work as a whole collection, not just as one book. If more people enter my series world and buy the next books, if more people join my email newsletter and potentially buy future releases, then **a free book is an asset that only grows my influence**.

You can make a book free on Kobo and iBooks and then report the lower price to Amazon in order to get it price matched. You can also offer it for free on your site.

Price per international market

If you self-publish direct to the main ebook retail stores, you can price in multiple currencies. NookPress has USD,

GBP and EUR, Kobo and Amazon have more currencies, e.g. CAD, AUD, INR and Apple allows for currency variation by country and region. If you don't price individually per region, but let the platform default the price, you will get odd pricing e.g. US$4.99 might turn up as £3.41 in the UK, whereas you might want the book to be £2.99. Pricing is also much more competitive in the UK than it is in, say, Australia, where the price of books is considerably higher.

Part 6: Marketing

6.1 Definition

It is no longer remarkable to write a book. Yes, you should celebrate your personal achievement, but there are millions of books and millions of authors out there, so what makes you and your books stand out?

We live in a crowded world and you have to get attention for your business somehow. Marketing is about getting noticed, so the customer can then make a decision about whether to buy your book. These days, that attention has to be earned.

For an in-depth look at marketing, I've written a full-length book on the topic, *How to Market a Book*, which covers everything in detail, so this section just contains an overview. I'll go through the three main approaches to marketing:

- **Book-based** – including book covers and your sales page on the distributors

- **Author-based** – including your website and author platform as well as social media

- **Customer-based** – reaching target audiences through media

Plus, I'll outline some key concepts and my own tale of two author brands in case you're making decisions around splitting your audience by writing in multiple genres.

6.2 Key concepts

Some authors feel that marketing is icky and they hate even the idea of it. But there are a few key concepts that will help you reframe marketing in a positive light.

Attraction marketing

People think marketing is spammy and sucky when it's focused around pushing all the time: Pushing out emails and social media that say "buy my book." Pushing out advertising to interrupt people's leisure time.

But marketing can be based around attraction, and that's been my own focus. Over the last five years. I've been creating content that people might enjoy or find interesting, for example, my blog posts, YouTube videos, podcast and sharing interesting stuff on social media around my niche. **In my worldview, marketing is sharing what you love with people who want to hear about it**. So if I share an article on ways to market audiobooks on my blog, it should be useful enough to be shared, which brings people to my site, and then they might sign up for my email list or buy a product from me.

Permission marketing and the email list

The phrase 'permission marketing' was coined by Seth Godin in his book of the same name, and essentially means that people give you permission to contact them. Their permission comes by giving you their email in exchange for a free ebook or signing up on your site. It might be by Liking your Facebook page or following you on Twitter. Building up an email list of people interested in your work is one of the most effective ways to reach people, and the best way is to have them opt in themselves.

As consumers, most of us don't give permission to be interrupted these days. We don't want ads in the middle of our TV programs, so we binge watch boxsets. We don't want cold callers on the phone at 7pm so we block our numbers. There are laws to prevent spammers from targeting us.

Treat people as you want to be treated. Don't add people to your email list manually. Make sure they do it themselves so you have their permission.

Generosity, social karma and co-opetition

The word karma implies that you get back what you give, and I believe this is true in the social environment. If you give, you will receive. Being useful, helpful and generous is satisfying to you personally, but also builds up a bank of goodwill. When you later mention that you have a book out, or people are attracted to you because of your generosity and see that you have books/products available, they are more likely to buy.

This isn't woo-woo. It's based on the science of influence. Read Robert Cialdini's book, *Influence*, and you'll understand that the principle of reciprocity is one of the keys to influencing people's behavior (in the nicest possible way!). We can utilize such principles, but we don't have to do it in a scammy or unethical manner.

Co-opetition is cooperating with your perceived competition so that both parties benefit. When there is a congruence of interests, cooperating together can create greater value than acting alone.

The self-publishing environment in particular is full of authors with entrepreneurial spirit, sharing openly. We discuss sales numbers and promote each other through blog posts and social networks, especially when our books are in the same genre. In working and educating ourselves together, we can learn lessons faster, respond and adapt more quickly.

6.3 Book-based marketing

If the product is no good, no amount of marketing will get it to sell consistently over time. Of course, the definition of 'good' is subjective, as evidenced by the prize-winning literary fiction that sells less than a thousand copies, and the massive commercial success of books like *Twilight* and *50 Shades of Grey*.

People like what they like, and there is room for many more kinds of books in this new online world.

Regardless of the genre you write in, the most important thing for marketing is that the fundamentals of your book are optimized. Here are the top things to consider.

- **Write a book you would like to read** and **use a professional editor** to make it the best book it can be.

- Use a **great cover design** that resonates with your target audience. It should give them an idea as to the type of book they're getting and hook them with a hint of what's inside. Here's a list of book cover designers that might help: thecreativepenn.com/bookcoverdesign/

- **If it's non-fiction, give it a search engine optimized (SEO) title**. People who read non-fiction are often looking for an answer to a specific problem. For example, my book *How to Market a Book*, doesn't have a clever title – it has an obvious title, because it does what it says on the box. You can discover what people are searching for by using the Amazon search bar. Start typing something in and it will auto-complete your words with the most common keywords or phrases.

- Use a **sales description** that actually makes people want to read the book. If it's non-fiction, you should be indicating what problem you're solving, or what benefit people will get from reading it. If it's fiction, then the main characters should be featured and a hint of the plot shown in the text. Questions that hook the reader can help get the audience involved in the book.

- Understand where the book fits on the bookshelf and **identify the correct category** for it within the publishing platforms. Everyone thinks their book is unique in some way, but every book also has to be loaded into the publishing computer systems, and so you have to choose a category. If you self-publish, you get two categories on Amazon, three or more on Kobo, Nook and Apple iBooks.

- **Use appropriate keywords in your metadata**. The Amazon auto-complete can also be used for identifying keywords and they can also be used to get you into other categories on Amazon.

- **Use pricing strategies appropriate to your market, genre and the length of the book**. Pricing is a marketing tool, and self-publishers have the opportunity to change pricing when they like. Permafree with the first in a series is one example of a pricing strategy, with subsequent books at higher prices. Non-fiction that has a specific value to the reader can usually be priced higher than fiction.

- Provide **multiple formats** for your work, e.g. ebook, print and audiobook, as you will reach different readers in those ways.

- Decide whether you want to use exclusivity. If not, make sure that your book is **available in all markets,**

on all platforms, as you'll reach different people on each. You'll also find new readers globally, so don't just publish in the US and in no other territory. If you have sold some of your rights, check the contracts to see which territories you might be able to self-publish in. For example, if you have sold UK and Commonwealth rights, you can self-publish in the US, and vice versa.

*   **Make sure your ebook has a good sample**, which is generally the first 10% of an ebook. Move any extraneous material to the end so that you can hook the reader at the beginning.

Other things to consider are:

*   **Write in a series.** Once readers are engaged in a series, they want to return to those characters and that world repeatedly, especially if you move people emotionally and include high stakes. Series are quicker to write as you don't have to invent from scratch.

*   **Write books of different lengths**. Long books were more important in a time when the size of the spine mattered. Digital reading and online print book sales mean that book length is less important and in fact, shorter works are popular in an age of decreased attention. Fiction authors are experimenting with novellas, typically 20,000-40,000 words, as well as short stories of around 5,000 words. Writing a variety of lengths can be a great way to satisfy readers more quickly or create new products to use as marketing. Non-fiction is getting shorter, with more people writing multiple shorter books, rather than one great opus.

- **Publish regularly.** You'll notice that none of the above involves blogging, social media, or TV/radio/ newspaper appearances. In fact, many of the top-earning authors these days get most of their sales through a regular publishing schedule that means their books take up a lot more digital shelf space. They also take advantage of the Amazon search algorithms that include a 30-day or 90-day bucket for new releases. Romance writer HM Ward released her novellas every 2.5 weeks in 2013 and has sold over 4 million books as well as making the *New York Times* list 13 times. Of course, most of us will struggle to write that fast, but regular publication is a marketing technique, just like the others on this list. You can use it or leave it aside, as you like.

- **Pay for promotion to specific book audiences**. Reader-focused sites like BookBub.com have email lists that are segmented into genres/categories. If your book meets certain criteria, it can feature in targeted emails to readers who have opted in to be notified of sales. This is often a great way to spike sales.

6.4 Author-based marketing

This aspect of marketing focuses on you as the author, and it's all about attracting people. This is the essence of the 'author platform' – if people find you, they will then discover your books and may go on to buy them if something resonates with them. Here are some of the aspects of platform:

- **Website and email list.** You need at least an author hub where you can have book pages and information about you, as well as any media and contact information. This is also the best place to have some kind of email list signup, which gives you the ability to tell customers about your next book when it comes out. Not so long ago you needed to know about programming to set up your own website, or you needed to pay someone several thousand dollars to do it for you. With the wide availability of free WordPress software and other easy-to-use platforms, it's pretty easy to set up and maintain your own site – if you're willing to give the technology a try! Budget a day or two to play around and you'll save yourself a lot of money over the longer term. I also recommend you try to find design themes that don't need major amounts of customization, as opposed to paying someone to design your site from scratch. I guarantee that you will change your mind over design, whatever you use upfront, and you will change your site every couple of years anyway, so there's no point in paying too much!

- **Blogging.** You certainly don't have to blog in order to sell books – it's just one of the many options. Many very successful authors don't blog at all. But personally, blogging changed my life. It freed up my writing style, it gave me a community and friendships, it enabled me to create multiple streams of income – and it does help to sell my books, especially my non-fiction. Maybe you're even reading this because you found me through my blog!

- **Multimedia – podcast/YouTube.** People connect with people, and your smile, your eyes, your voice, laugh and mannerisms can make a huge difference in how people feel about you. We are more than words on a page – we are real people. It's true that authors are usually more interesting on the page than they are in real life, but we can still use multimedia to our advantage. Try podcasting, or doing videos on YouTube as an experiment. You might just like it.

- **Social media**. There are so many options with social media, but at heart, it's a way to communicate with people and have conversations. It's a way to connect with readers and other authors. It's a way to demonstrate you're a real person by sharing interesting, entertaining or inspiring things and giving a glimpse into your world. It's also a way to attract a global audience, since Facebook, Twitter, Pinterest, LinkedIn and all the rest are global networks. Find what you enjoy and focus your energy there.

- **Speaking** is a great way to attract readers. Again, it's about personal connection, as people will hear your voice and your personality will come across in how you perform. If you're engaging when you speak, or read your work, people will be more interested in hearing from you. I cover this topic in detail in my book, *Public Speaking for Authors, Creatives and Other Introverts.*

- **Existing business.** You may already have a business, and this can be the basis of your author platform. This is particularly common in the non-fiction area, e.g. a communications consultant writing a book on effective communication can sell it to their clients.

6.5 Customer-based marketing

The third aspect of your marketing focuses on the customer for your specific book, which may differ between books or series. It focuses on meeting the customer where they are, whether it's through traditional media avenues, online, or in person. Go back and review Part 4.2 Who are your customers before going through this section as it expands on that chapter.

Who are your customers? What do they like?

Now you can get more specific about demographic information around gender and age. Are they an eco-conscious Mum of two young kids? A 20-something tech-focused young male gamer? A Boomer grandparent with one eye on maximizing their pension before retirement and the other on the next exotic holiday?

Personally, I think outlook on life can be more important, and you can spin the angle of your book based on these aspects. For example, someone who lives in a multicultural city anywhere in the world might enjoy my thriller *Desecration* as it's set in London with a mixed race character. People who think there's more than just the physical realm may enjoy the psychic ideas, regardless of their age or gender.

Consider who might enjoy aspects of your book. For example, a book that features scenes in India may have a bigger audience amongst expat Indians living abroad, or people who love India (like me!).

What do they read? Or watch? Where do they hang out?

The young gamer might read *Wired* magazine on his smart phone and participate in gaming forums. He also goes to ComicCon. The eco-conscious Mum buys organic gardening books but also chick-lit for escapism, as well as frequenting MumsNet for the latest kids' books and up-to-date health stuff. She likes to buy local or from the artist's website directly. The Boomer is reading the latest business books to stay relevant, but is also reading the expanding range of Boomer blogs and listening to podcasts about the third stage of life. Both the Mum and the Boomer grandparent are interested in books for kids. If you profile your target market like this, thinking about demographics, interests and lifestyle, you'll be able to consider where to reach them in more detail.

Once you have an idea of who might like your books, you can then go about targeting them where they hang out.

Target specifically

Perhaps you've written a techno-thriller that will appeal to that young gamer, and you want to feature in *Wired* magazine – which generally doesn't talk about fiction. The best way to do this is:

- **Read the publication** you're aiming at so you understand its style, or watch/listen to the show. You have to understand what the publication/show wants before you pitch.

- **Identify specific journalists** who have written about similar topics or who seem open to your niche interest. Consume what they do, read their blog and their tweets. Be helpful to them if you can, retweet them, leave a comment before you ask for anything. Cyber stalk them in a totally non-threatening way, so you get to know how they work. You can also register on a site like HelpAReporter.com and wait for opportunities.

- **Decide on a story angle** – and remember, the story is NEVER that you have written a book. It might be something related to your research, some new technology that tangentially relates to your book, some data point that will interest the readers/listeners/viewers. You are merely the expert on this topic, and you're not pitching your book, only the story behind it – it's understood that, if featured, your byline will include the name of the book, and hopefully your website.

This micro-targeting is much more effective than the scattergun effect of mass media. The latter is generally pointless and won't result in sales for most authors, especially if your book is not in bookstores. I've been on national TV and radio several times and haven't seen any additional sales at all. There are even cases of authors appearing on Oprah and having no significant sales spike, since the book just didn't resonate with that particular audience.

It's always more useful to have clickable links on a site with a targeted audience, so online blog posts, articles, show notes on podcasts and any online media are preferable, as they can have a direct link to your book sales page, email list signup or website.

Remember: the whole point is to resonate with a particular audience in some way so that they go on to discover your book.

6.6 A tale of two author brands

I write under two author names: Joanna Penn for non-fiction and J.F.Penn for my fiction. I maintain two websites and several different variations of social media, which is a lot of work! Many authors want to know whether this type of split is entirely necessary, and of course, it's really a decision you have to make for your own business.

Here's an outline of my two brands and how they contribute to my business, as well as my recommendations if you're thinking about these issues.

What is a brand, anyway?

Whether you like it or not, you have a brand as soon as you publish a book, or you start tweeting, or blogging, or putting yourself out there in any way online and off.

It's how people perceive you. It's the words and images that are associated with you and your books. It's the emotions and feelings you trigger in the person who notices you or something you put into the world. If you write a book for public consumption, you have to accept that this is inevitable.

Therefore, it's important to control the perception of your brand. You can do that by making sure that everything you put out there in the world represents what you want people to see.

TheCreativePenn.com – and me as Joanna Penn

- My main website, TheCreativePenn.com, is aimed at writers, authors and those who are, or want to be, creative entrepreneurs. The tone is upbeat and I want to be a positive force for good, so I only share what resonates with that vibe. Of course, I have down days like everyone else, but I don't share those openly.

- The site makes income through the sale of online courses, non-fiction books, professional speaking, affiliate income, and sponsorship of the podcast.

- I blog every week and continue to put out quality podcast interviews, video on my YouTube channel and use social media to drive traffic. I love serving my audience but TheCreativePenn.com was always intended to be a business, so I keep that in mind.

- The color scheme is red and white, the tone and website style is positive, upbeat, helpful and smiley, and that is a part of who I really am authentically. But it's only one aspect.

JFPenn.com – and me as J.F.Penn

- I write fiction under J.F.Penn, and JFPenn.com is targeted at fans of that work, or people who might like to try my type of books. The tag line is *Thrillers on the edge* because I find myself writing on the edge of thriller, mystery, supernatural suspense, and crime, with a healthy dose of literary and cultural references.

- The tone and website style is dark, my picture is dark and brooding (no smiling!) and the color scheme is black, greys and white. This resonates because my fiction is dark and twisty, and my themes are religion, psychology, the supernatural, as well as global travel, and fascinating locations. I talk with other thriller, horror and crime writers about our obsessions on my occasional video interviews. The primary function of the site is an author hub with all the information about my fiction, as well as email list signups driven mostly by directing people to a link at the back of my books. The tone is quite different to TheCreativePenn – that's also me but, again, only one aspect.

- The income on JFPenn.com is purely from the sales of my fiction, which continues to grow as a percentage of my overall income. The site itself is mainly marketed through the books themselves, interviews I do on book blogs, as well as podcasts and social media.

Why do I have two brands?

I started TheCreativePenn.com as a way to share my self-publishing learning curve, way back in 2008 when there was no international Kindle, no KDP or Createspace. I'd made some huge mistakes, including printing too much inventory without knowing anything about marketing, and I was really keen to share my story so that others could avoid that pain. I also saw my future as a non-fiction author and speaker, empowering people with live events and online training. A bit like a British Tony Robbins!

(a) I didn't ever expect to write fiction when I started The Creative Penn in Dec 2008

It truly didn't enter my consciousness, until this interview with Tom Evans in June 2009 about writer's blocks - http://bit.ly/WcGhzk - when we uncovered my own blocks around writing fiction. After that discussion, I moved forward, starting NaNoWriMo in Nov 2009. You can read the whole journey of writing my first novel here: http://bit.ly/1qcFjiC.

But essentially, the original goal for TheCreativePenn.com never had anything to do with fiction! I had originally set my path towards becoming a full-time blogger/entrepreneur, and that didn't change until 2011 when I realized being a fiction author was a possible future for me, and now it's my primary goal alongside the non-fiction work.

By the way, if you're writing fiction, and you want to start a blog, then start a blog that attracts your target audience! Don't do what I am doing – unless, like me, you have a goal for your writer site that relates to income or marketing. Or, of course, you can write what you want if you just write for the fun of it (which is absolutely valid, but you probably won't put in the kind of hours I do if it's just for fun!)

In terms of learning from my 'mistakes,' I basically had to start from scratch with JFPenn.com when I changed direction, because such a small percentage of my non-fiction audience are interested in my fiction. If I was starting again today and aiming to make 100% of my money from fiction, I would continue blogging as I do occasionally at JFPenn.com about my research, videos about the books and interviews with other authors in the genre. I would rarely talk about the writing process, and I would never talk about publishing or marketing. Primarily, I would focus on publishing fiction more regularly. But because I maintain this split business model, I need the two sites, and they continue to satisfy both sides of my personality.

(b) Different target audiences

The target market for TheCreativePenn.com and my non-fiction books is very different from the people who want to read my fiction and check out JFPenn.com. Yes, some will cross over, but I have found it to be a small percentage.

To attract a specific target market, you need to focus on specific topics they want so that they feel at home when they arrive at your site. You also need to build separate email lists for the different audiences.

You can separate your audience for your books through a different author name, as you can have separate author pages on Amazon, Kobo and the other book retailers so that readers only see the books associated with that name.

I did start out with Joanna Penn for all of my books but differentiating the target market soon became important, as did …

(c) The gender issue with my type of fiction

After *Pentecost* and then *Prophecy*, when some of my readers came from TheCreativePenn.com and knew me as the smiley, happy person, I received feedback that my writing was 'masculine,' and that my gender was causing people to double take at the kickass characters in my books.

A lot of writers use initials to get over this kind of instinctive gender bias, and so I decided to move to J.F.Penn in order to prevent people judging the books before they'd even read a sentence. I've written a much longer article on the gender bias issue here: http://bit.ly/1u18Hcw.

When are multiple brands recommended?

If you can avoid multiple brands, then it's advisable to try and stick with one. It's very hard to be active with more than one brand, for example, I gave up trying to tweet under two handles, so I use @thecreativepenn for everything.

I don't podcast on JFPenn although I do record some of my short stories in audio. I have a separate Facebook page but I'm not terribly active there. I have Pinterest boards for JFPenn and not for TheCreativePenn, but I am on Google Plus as Joanna Penn. I have two sets of business cards, two email addresses, two different official photos (one smiling, one brooding!)

Aaaaaargghhh … it's complicated!

But I'm glad I did it, as I feel the need to keep my two audiences separate and that's the main reason why you would want two such separate brands.

You can use multiple author names and still only have one website, of course, but if you write children's fiction AND horror, then you'll definitely want two sites. But if you write thrillers and romance, you could probably get away with one brand.

Questions to ask yourself around whether you should use multiple brands

- Who is my target audience for these types of books, or this type of site?

- Where do I want to be in 5 years' time? Can this brand grow with me? For example, your name will always last, whereas a site based on one book may not as you write more over time.

- Can I get away with just being one brand? *(as this is much easier and I highly advise you to do this unless you definitely need to keep your audiences apart)*

- How do I want people to perceive me?

- How can I communicate that in what I create in the world?

Part 7: Financials

7.1 Definition

"Finance is the art and science of watching the money flowing into and out of a business, then deciding how to allocate it and determining whether or not what you're doing is producing the results you want."

Josh Kaufman, **The Personal MBA**

If your writing is more than a hobby, then it's important to actively manage the financial side of things. In this section, we tackle the money mindset, where your revenue comes from and how to increase it, as well as costs and funding for your business, plus the practical side of banking, accounting, reporting and tax.

Trust me, it will be more fun than it sounds!

7.2 Money mindset

Your mindset is critical when it comes to money and management of it, and that includes reporting, tax obligations, working with accountants, and more. Here are some of the things I've heard from authors when I talk about this type of thing:

- I'm just no good at numbers, so I ignore all that.

- I hate talking about money/accounting/reporting/ tax – it's so boring.

- I want to make lots of money, but I want someone else to handle it.

- I don't know what my expenses are.

- I don't know how much income I get per month for book sales; I don't know how much profit I make.

- I can't be bothered filling in withholding tax exemption forms – It's too complicated.

- My agent deals with the money side; I'm just grateful to get cash in my bank account.

It's time to change your mindset

I'm not getting all woo-woo or law of attraction on you here. We're not talking about manifesting millions in your bank account just by thinking about it. But certainly, if you're not excited about making money, then don't complain when you don't make any. If you're not bothered about tracking your money, then don't complain if it goes astray.

If you can't be bothered to learn the basics of accounting, tax and reporting, then how will you understand how to make more income, or learn to reduce your expenses in order to make more profit?

If you don't want to bother with those withholding tax forms for foreign income, then don't complain when ~30% of your income is left in the government accounts of other countries. If you're no good at numbers, then perhaps it's time to start learning!

If you let someone else have control over your money, you could also be in for a shock. Most agents and publishers are scrupulous about accounting, but there are a number of horror stories about literary agents embezzling from their clients, including Harper Lee's agent for *To Kill a Mockingbird*. If you sign an agency agreement that means the agent gets paid by the publisher first, then you have already lost control. Read this article on Agents and Money from Kristine Kathryn Rusch for more detail: http://bit.ly/Z7mjYA.

Basically, you need to invest a little time in your financial education in order to understand this stuff. It's not rocket science.

If you really have no clue at all, I recommend:

- *Rich Dad, Poor Dad* – Robert Kiyosaki. The fundamentals of money told in a story format.

- *Rich Dad's Cashflow Quadrant* – Robert Kiyosaki. This book will help you to understand why being a business owner is such a great idea, and why creating assets is the way forward.

7.3 Income circles exercise

In Part 1, we looked at your definition of success on a larger scale. Now we've tackled the bigger goals, it's time to get more specific around money and income. This exercise is a simple way to express your current reality, as well as reflecting on your future desired state. You'll need a pen and paper and there is a space for this in the Companion Workbook on the Download page.

(1) Draw circle/s reflecting your income sources right now

Five years ago, when I first did this exercise, I just had one big circle – my day job as a business consultant. Perhaps you have that main one, and perhaps a smaller one with interest on a savings account, perhaps you have a rental property, perhaps you're making a little trickle of money from your writing already.

Whatever your reality is right now, draw your own circles, and if you have a partner/spouse, draw circles for your household. Be honest: no one will see it!

(2) Think about what the circles mean for you and your family

Consider the following:

- How much security is there versus risk in your income streams?

- What happens if your major income stream disappears or lessens?

- What are the downstream dependencies of that income stream, e.g. mortgage, school fees, health?

(3) Draw circles to reflect what you would like your income sources to be in five years' time

You'll need to make this up entirely! You can aim for whatever you like, but you can definitely achieve a huge amount in that length of time. You can choose to keep the overall size of your income the same, but split it into different circles. You can make some circles bigger than others.

When I drew my future circles five years ago, I had the same amount of overall money split into broad categories:

- Book sales

- Professional speaking

- Courses/product sales

- Affiliate income

I also had my circles approximately the same sizes, as I had no real inkling of what my future might look like, only that I didn't want that one big circle running my life. Now, I split my circles into the retailers who sell my books and pay me monthly or quarterly – Amazon, Kobo, Apple, Nook, Audible, Createspace – plus the direct sales I make from my own website, but essentially, my multiple circle future is now a reality. So it can happen!

(4) Reflect on the differences between the two versions

Perhaps you have more circles in the second version, reflecting the desire NOT to be dependent on one source for income streams.

Perhaps you have some circles bigger than others, reflecting your personal preferences for what you enjoy doing.

Perhaps your day job still features, but is a smaller size, with income from writing appearing as a smaller bubble next to it.

Write down the reasons behind your choices for these future circles.

(5) What do you have to do to reach that future circle state?

If you want to get to the reality of those future circles, what do you need to do?

For example, I assume that one of those circles will be book sales – so you need to write some books. If one of the circles is from public speaking, as mine has always been, then you need to improve your speaking ability, do a lot more speaking and start charging more. If you have direct sales, or affiliate sales (commission from the sale of other people's products), then you'll need a website, or a newsletter, or a mechanism for sale.

Thinking along these lines will help you become more specific over time. Your future circles can also become a kind of vision statement, a graphical representation of your future state.

7.4 Revenues of the author business

If you don't get paid, it's not a business! Running a creative business means that you have to think about where your money will come from.

Authors create assets in the form of books and other products. An asset is "anything tangible or intangible that is capable of being owned or controlled to produce value and that is held to have positive economic value" (Wikipedia).

So our assets, our books, bring us positive economic value (income), usually from the following sources.

From distributors

You can only reach a specific number of people on your own, so many of us use distributors to reach a wider audience for our work.

If you self-publish, it will be sites like Amazon, Apple for iBookstore, Kobo, Nook or a site like Smashwords, Draft-2Digital or BookBaby.

Each of these have different payment terms which you need to be aware of in order to track expected income. For example, this could be 60 days following the end of the calendar month of sales direct deposit to your bank account or quarterly by PayPal.

From publishers

Many authors are now hybrid, in that they combine traditional publishing with self-publishing. If you sign a traditional publishing deal, you may receive an advance against royalties, an upfront payment that is usually split into several parts. You may get one part on signing, one on delivering the final manuscript, and another part on publication. Once that advance is earned out, which means that the book sales have covered the initial advance, then you may also receive royalties in the future.

Most publishers issue royalty payments every quarter or six months, with a statement that breaks down what the royalty covers.

Directly from individuals who purchase your work

If you do sell direct to customers, you will usually collect money directly at the time of purchase.

For example:

- Book sales through your own website as per section 5.3 Selling direct.

- Consulting fees can be paid in advance of services or afterwards. I confirm the appointment time for consulting after payment through PayPal, and offer a 100% money-back guarantee if people feel they haven't gained value for money.

- If you sell your work at speaking events, you will likely take cash from customers. For accounting purposes, I usually total up the cash and then do a transfer from my personal account to my business account online for the total amount and call it 'Income – Book Sales.' You can also pay in the cash after the event. However you do it, it's important to account for that kind of income so that you can track it.

- Kickstarter, IndieGoGo and other crowdfunding sources are another way to be paid directly from customers. However, it's important to be aware that these sites depend on your existing fans and you're unlikely to get funded if you're starting from scratch. More on this in 7.8 Funding your business.

From affiliate commission sales

Affiliate income is a common source for anyone with a well-trafficked website or an ability to reach an audience directly. Essentially, you promote someone else's service/ product and if people buy, then you receive a percentage commission.

I'm an affiliate of Amazon and iBooks, as well as some of the tools I use for my own site like Aweber, and services that I have used and can personally recommend. You are usually paid monthly by PayPal, check or bank transfer.

From companies you freelance for

Many creatives will freelance for companies, e.g. teaching or doing art directly for them or freelance writing. For example, I speak professionally several times a year for various companies. After the event, I send an invoice to the finance department, who usually have a standard payment terms of 30 days. One company I worked for didn't pay me for four months despite me chasing them up. If you have an issue of non-payment, try not to work for that company again.

Companies will have different payment terms and different requirements for invoicing, e.g. a purchase order number, or specific approvals. It's important to stay on top of follow-up to avoid non-payment.

Track your income correctly

You need to know when the money is coming in from all these sources so that you can calculate cash-flow. It's also good for your own reporting to understand the split of your income and you can do that through your accounting structure, explained in more detail in the accounting section.

In terms of my income statement, I separate income into the following accounts:

- Book royalties, which is further split by customer e.g. Amazon, Kobo, Apple, Nook, direct sales

- Affiliate commission, further split by customer e.g. Amazon, Aweber, etc.

- Product sales, generally my online courses

- Speaking

- Sponsorship/advertising

Income vs. profit

Of course, income is just one measure. Once you take out costs, you are (hopefully) left with profit. Your business is not profitable if your expenses exceed your income. Most businesses start out running at a loss, because it takes some time to see the revenue from your work.

How much profit you want will be related to your definition of success. Paul Graham, venture capitalist and founder of startup incubator, Y Combinator, talks about 'ramen profitable.' That's the level of profit that enables you to pay the basic rent and bills, as long as you eat basic food like ramen. You're happy enough with the business at that level if you can do what you want to do with your time. From there, you can define the amount of money you are comfortable living on.

How long will it take for the business to become profitable?

"It is unusual, and indeed abnormal, for a concern to make money during the first several years of its existence. The initial product and initial organization are never right."

Harvey S. Firestone, **Founder of the Firestone Tire and Rubber Company**

I've started a number of businesses and most of them were never profitable. I ploughed my own savings into these ventures with the expectation of a return at some point, but for various reasons, those businesses didn't work out. (Much more on that in my book, *Career Change.*)

The Creative Penn, which I ran part time for the first three years, was profitable from around year two, when I had enough assets to bring in adequate income to offset my expenses. I only resigned from my day job in year three and even then, the profit was not substantial. I'm now coming into year five and the profit is decent but I'm not an uber-indie outlier as yet. (Give me time!)

As with any financial plan, you can only make rough guesses as to what might happen. But that's OK, it's what publishers do with any book. You have to put your stake in the ground and move it later based on actual results.

Here are some other things to consider when you are working out how long it will take for your author business to be profitable:

- **The average book sells between 250 - 3,000 copies in its lifetime.** The figures vary by genre, language and by study, but the reality is that most books don't sell that many copies, however they are published. We generally only hear about the outliers. But the good news for indie authors is that even if you sell one book a day, that will add up over the many years you own your own rights. And of course, we're not aiming to be average!

- **Certain types of books are more popular and will sell more copies**. For example, most romance books will always sell more than literary fiction. Check out the Author Earnings reports (authorearnings.com/reports/) for details on which genres sell the most copies. Of course, you don't necessarily want to write to the market, but you do need to be realistic about sales figures for your genre.

- Like any industry, **earnings are not spread equally across all authors**. Some authors will be earning megabucks, and others will be barely scraping by. Nobody said life was fair! You just have to write the best books you can, write lots of them and keep connecting with readers. As Hugh Howey says, **the real story of self-publishing is not the authors making multi-six figure sums, but the sheer number of authors making enough to pay even a small number of bills**.

The point is that, unless lightning strikes, you need to put in the time to create the assets (books and products) that create the income and keep your expenses down so that you can make a profit.

Do some basic calculations

You can play around with the figures, and it's all based on best guess, but here's something to start you off:

- 1 book priced at $2.99, self-published for 70% royalty makes $2 per copy. Estimated sale = 100 per month = 1,200 copies per year. Total income per annum (p.a.) = $2,400

- If you budget $1000 for editing and cover design, your profit will be $1,400 in the first year and then $2,400 p.a. going forward (assuming sales stay equal)

- You will need 10 books selling at this rate to make $24,000 p.a. Most people would agree that even this isn't enough to live well on, in the US or Europe at least. To increase that, you either need more books, or more copies sold of each, or a higher profit per book, or multiple income streams.

Once you increase your number of income streams, the little trickles can soon add up, but it's important to start off being realistic about the likelihood of making lots of money quickly. From a personal perspective, I know that this business model works, but it takes time and effort and lots of production to get to a decent level of income!

7.5 Increase your revenue

Derek Sivers sold his company CD Baby and now sells ebooks about starting a business in foreign markets at Woodegg.com. I read this article from him about how to increase cash-flow in a business - http://bit.ly/1u1agr2 - and it struck home as true for authors as well.

There are four basic ways to increase your revenue:

(1) Increase the number of customers you serve

This can be done by expanding your customer base through publishing on multiple platforms. Although Amazon's KDP Select program offers benefits, it limits your sales to people who buy on that particular platform. They may dominate in the US and UK, but Kobo dominates in Canada, and iBooks dominates in many other global markets. I recently published *Pentecost* and *Desecration-Verletzung* in German, and in Germany there is a challenger to Kindle in the Tolino reader, which has 40% of the market so is not to be ignored when publishing.

You can also increase the number of customers served by offering your books in multiple formats – ebook, print and audiobook – as well as in multiple countries. You can also consider translation to reach people in different languages.

(2) Increase the average size of the transaction by selling more

This can be done by having multiple books that customers might like within product lines. If a customer buys one book and enjoys it, they are likely to want more. This is why many authors write in a series, and why many publishers prefer books in a series.

If you have more books available, the customer may buy more. The power is in the backlist, which is why being an author is a long-term game. At the London Book Fair 2014, I talked to Barbara Freethy, who has over 35 books and, as I write this, is the bestselling KDP author of all time with over 4.5 million books sold. She mentioned that when someone new discovers her books, she sees an overall effect as they dive into her backlist.

Bundling is another way to do this. You can do ebook boxsets as a single author and charge more for a single transaction, which is also a great deal for the customer. For example, I sell ARKANE Books 1-3, *Pentecost*, *Prophecy* and *Exodus*, in a box-set for $5.99. If bought separately, they would cost $9.98, so it's a good deal for everyone. All you need to do is create a file with multiple books in, and get a cover designed that looks like a boxset.

(3) Increase the frequency of transactions by customer

This can be done by releasing books and products more often, so that loyal customers return. It's important to use an email list to capture their information so that you can tell them when you have a new product available.

Some authors are doing this through serialization. H.M.Ward's Ferro series is a good example of this, currently with over 14 books in one particular series with many of them 20,000-30,000 word novellas.

Others are doing this through co-writing. For example, Jeremy Robinson's Jack Sigler Chess Team series has several co-authors writing in his world.

(4) Raise your prices

There are a couple of ways in which authors are doing this:

- **Charge more for all books.** When you're first start-ing out, you need to lower the barrier to entry so that people will try your books. But as you become more established and more people are aware of your books, you might find that people are happy to pay more.

- **Make the first book available for free and then raise the price of others in the series**. If you do the math right, you'll see that you can make more money this way than using a 99c entry price point.

- **Sell direct to loyal fans** through hardcover specials and limited editions. Scott Sigler does a galactic football league series that he self-publishes and sells direct. Cory Doctorow did some brilliant hand-bound hardcover editions of his book, *With a Little Help*.

7.6 Costs of the author business

"Watch the costs and the profits will
take care of themselves."

Andrew Carnegie

There are costs in any business, and it's important to be aware of the upfront costs as well as the ongoing costs.

I'm not an accountant, so this is just an overview of business from my point of view. Please see a professional for advice on your situation or any questions about specific accounting issues.

Your time

I'm including this here because time is the greatest cost for any of us. We only have a finite amount, and you could be using your time to earn money in a different way, or just enjoying life. Therefore, how you spend your time is critical. Three things that help me manage my time are:

- **Consciously choosing my strategy, business model and lifestyle goals**. I've changed business direction a number of times over the last few years, but in January 2014 I decided to transition to a primarily book-based income model, with professional speaking and affiliate income from my blog as secondary. This means that I have gradually changed my focus in terms of time towards writing more books and winding down the courses for authors that I used to teach. In terms of my lifestyle goals, when an opportunity presents itself, I ask questions to see if it fits. For example, does it fit my choice to be location independent? To travel more? Does it allow me to spend weekends with my husband? If the opportunity doesn't fit my stated goals, I say no.

- **Sign on my wall.** "Have you made art today? Have you written 1000 words? Are you a step closer?" This is a physical reminder of my primary goal which is creating new things in the world. I see that sign every day when I sit down at my desk and it keeps me honest with my time. I'm allowed to do email and marketing activities when I've achieved that goal. That's the theory of course, but like all of us, I don't achieve that every day!

- **Timesheet app.** I use OfficeTime app on my iPhone and track my hours every day as if I worked in a 'proper' company. It helps me keep accountable and if I see the 'Email and Social' time bucket creeping up over an hour a day, I know it's time to cut back. You can even take this a step further and assign an hourly rate to your time, calculating the cost of production for a book. I have buckets for Writing First Draft, Editing and then Publishing Tasks. I consider marketing tasks to be apportioned to all books, since it's generally about visibility overall.

Startup costs

I once ran a luxury scuba diving business in New Zealand. Before we even ran a trip there were huge outlays to consider – boat hire, scuba diving equipment, insurance, personnel costs for skipper and DiveMaster, plus the marketing to find customers. Authors are lucky, because our startup costs are very low.

- **Computer.** Whether this is a high spec desktop with a massive screen or a portable laptop, you generally need more than pen and paper to run your business as an author. I replace my laptop every three years or as soon as the speed starts to impact my efficiency. This hardware can be depreciated, which means the expense is apportioned over the life of the computer. You should also have an external drive or cloud storage to backup your work regularly, just in case!

- **Somewhere to write.** For most authors, this isn't a cost, as many write at home, or in cafes. Maybe factor in the price of a coffee or two! I belong to the members-only London Library, where I go several times a week to write. This is a paid subscription, but it gets me out of the house and keeps me from going completely barmy as a hermit writer!

- **Investment in your learning curve**. I believe everyone should have a budget for self-development. This may include books on writing, courses, conventions, or online products. For example, there are plenty of books on writing, how to self-publish effectively, and how to market a book. It will cost you very little to learn from others and avoid pain and heartache.

- **Professional editors and cover designers**. Whether you want a traditional publishing deal or you self-publish, a professional editor can help you make your book the best it can be. To publish your book, you will need a cover design, and a professional one is recommended unless you have graphic design skills specific to book design.

- **Smart phone.** This is obviously an optional extra, but I have found the smart phone to be a hugely valuable tool for my business. I keep ideas in the Things app, I use the social media apps to schedule on the go in little snatches of time, and I have brainstormed articles and books in text editor apps. I also take a lot of pictures for research or marketing purposes. I don't have email on my phone, as I found it became addictive, but I certainly think it saves me time. There's much more on the tools I use in my business in Appendix C.

Ensure that you have an initial budget

When you open your bank account for your business, you will have to enter a specific amount into the account as an initial deposit. I suggest that you look at the time it will take you to start to receive income and then calculate how much you will need for your initial expenses. Try and use this initial budget to keep tabs on your expenditure and yes, you may need to top this up over time.

Self-publishing as a business definitely involves initial outlay, as does any business, which is why it's best to start on the side while you work a day job.

Ongoing expenses

Here are some of the possible expenses you might incur on top of payroll, pension and dividends as covered under the Employee section. I've listed them in alphabetical order and of course, you may categorize things differently.

It's important to split out your costs so you can track them in a way that is meaningful for you. If you can track things, you can measure and control them. If you just had one big bucket for 'Expenses,' you wouldn't know what they were or what you were overspending on. Some of these are more controllable than others, e.g. you will always need to pay an accountant, bank charges and things like internet costs, but you can cut down on other expenditure like Office Supplies, Entertainment, Travel, etc.

- **Accounting fees**. Money you pay to your accountant, often annually.

- **Advertising/ promotional costs**. This includes paid promotions like BookBub, print costs and shipping for review copies of books, prizes for competitions, banner design for website advertising.

- **Bank charges**. I include PayPal fees in this bucket as well as bank charges for multi-currency transactions.

- **Commission.** I do some joint-venture projects and so I pay commissions for those sales, as well as affiliate commissions.

- **Computer hardware and software**. Your accountant will split your purchases into what is depreciable and what can be expensed. This may include purchases like a new laptop, Scrivener software for writing, Nuance Dragons speech to text, or a wireless mouse.

- **Entertainment.** Don't get too excited – the author's life is not about partying! In fact, there's very little partying! Most of my entertainment costs are coffee and meals out with other people for business purposes.

- **Internet costs.** This includes website and multimedia hosting, email list management, shopping cart fees. You can usually charge a percentage of your internet line, although it's worth asking your accountant how much.

- **Office supplies.** Includes stationery, print cartridges, business cards, and other basic office supplies.

- **Postage.** Mainly shipping books for giveaways, although yours might include shipping books that you've sold directly online.

- **Professional courses/training.** For example, I attend ThrillerFest in New York and the cost of the ticket goes into this expenses bucket. I also take quite a lot of online and in-person courses.

- **Professional fees.** For me, this is membership of Crime Writer's Association, The London Library and other professional bodies like the Alliance of Independent Authors.

- **Publishing costs**. This includes editing, book cover design, interior book design, and ordering print proof copies.

- **Research for books**. I do a lot of research trips for my books, so this includes the price of entry to exhibitions as well as purchasing books and materials that go into my study of the topic of the book.

- **Subsistence.** This accounts for meals alone on business trips rather than entertainment, which involves multiple people.

- **Tax.** This includes paying tax for employees as well as corporation tax and any other tax obligations.

- **Telephone**. Mobile calls and phone internet charges.

- **Travel.** For example, my flights to attend conventions, or train tickets for speaking events.

- **Virtual Assistant.** I now have a VA who helps me with some activities, so I have created a new expense code to track that cost specifically.

How do you split out your expenses at the moment? How could you improve your tracking of expenditure by splitting them out further? Check with your accountant if you're unclear on what counts as a company expense.

7.7 Funding your business

The author business barely has any startup costs and the ongoing costs are pretty minimal. But every startup needs some seed funding, and you do need a small budget to get going as an independent author.

My first novel cost me much more than subsequent ones, because the learning curve was so steep. I took professional writing courses. I paid three professional editors – a structural editor, a line editor and a proofreader – as well as a book designer. I paid for (pointless) printing and marketing stuff that I wouldn't recommend anymore.

How did I pay for that when I wasn't making any money from my books?

I had a day job. I also cut out the extraneous stuff from my life so that I could focus on my primary goal, which was getting out of that day job and becoming a creative entrepreneur. So I didn't have much social life, or any other hobbies. I spent any residual money on investing in my education and future business as a creative entrepreneur.

This is my advice to you, too – just save the money. Bootstrap your beginnings. You only need a little, and you can barter for many services if you have more time than cash. As you start to make sales, you can reinvest over time.

Crowdfunding

The popularity of crowdfunding has created some amazing success stories, but the reality for most is not so spectacular.

I'm going to be blunt here. Kickstarter, IndieGoGo and other crowdfunding tools are primarily for people with an established platform to create something cool and unusual that goes far beyond 'just a book.' There is one platform for writers specifically, Pubslush.com, but generally, at any of these sites, you will only get backing if you already have an audience to ask. Crowdfunding is not a way for a new author to get money to pay an editor and cover designer for their first book.

I join quite a few crowdfunding projects, but they are often unusual – or for people I am already fans of. Examples include: Seth Godin's *Icarus Deception*, which was a book, but also included a mega-oversize hardback and loads of extra goodies; a font created from Sigmund Freud's handwriting and the Morbid Anatomy Museum in New York.

Another consideration with crowdfunding is the number of people you will be accountable to if you're funded. One of my attractions to being an independent author is the freedom to create what I want, publish when I want and travel when I like – without asking permission. I can also change my mind, which inevitably happens when the book doesn't quite turn out as I thought. I'm not writing crowdfunding off, but I'd only do it for the right project.

If you want to try crowdfunding, here are a couple of useful articles about the challenges:

- Anatomy of a successful Kickstarter campaign (and what you should know before launching yours) by Tom Allen on crowdfunding his first book project - http://bit.ly/1qcJ1sD

- A warts-and-all guide to Kickstarter: What works and what doesn't (plus where we royally screwed up) by Sean Platt and Johnny B. Truant on crowdfunding Fiction Unboxed, writing and publishing a story in a month in public - http://bit.ly/1undT9X

7.8 Banking and PayPal

You need to have some basic setup in place in order to receive income and pay expenses.

Your business bank account

Set up a separate account for your business, whether or not you have a registered company, as, if you are taking this career seriously, you need to track income and expenses. It's very easy to lose track of how much you're spending if you aren't keeping separate accounts.

I have several business bank accounts:

- **Main transactional account.** This is where the money goes in and out of most of the time. I move money out of here to my accrual account every month.

- **Accrual account.** An accrual is basically an accumulation of money for things you will have to pay for in the future. For businesses, this is mainly tax, but it can also include money you are saving for your business e.g. a research trip, editing, or equipment you need to grow your business, e.g. a new laptop.

- **USD account.** I am in the UK and so my other accounts are in GBP, but I also have a USD account to pay in USD checks I receive from mainly affiliate sources. I transfer this periodically to my main GBP account and the exchange rate is calculated on the day of transfer. I also pay my US editor from this account.

PayPal

These days, you will likely need some way of paying and receiving money online. It used to be that businesses required a merchant account with a bank with exorbitant fees to take credit card payments, but now you can use PayPal, or other similar services to send and receive money in multiple currencies with charges that are reasonable and which are much easier to use.

This does take a little setup time, so allow a few weeks before you're fully operational. You need to set up a PayPal account in your country, and enter the required details. You will then need to scan and send verified documents to prove your identity, part of anti-terrorism and anti-money laundering procedures. Once that is all sorted, you can link your bank account so that you can 'download' money to your 'real' bank. You can also now get PayPal debit and credit cards to allow you to use money from the account directly.

Once the account is verified, it works very well, and can then be used to sell books, products, and services online as well as integrating with event sites like Eventbrite and other shopping carts. The transfer from PayPal to your bank account usually happens on the same day, unless there are flags on your account for some reason. If you're doing a big launch and expect mass transactions through PayPal, this can often cause your account to be flagged, so it's a good idea to use it over a longer period of time to build up a reputation before you get lots of transactions through it in a short period.

I account for my PayPal transactions as if the various currencies are bank accounts, so I have PayPal USD and PayPal GBP set up in my QuickBooks accounting software alongside my main bank accounts.

All of these accounts have fees associated with them. This is a cost of doing business and, of course, you can compare international fees per bank, but you will be paying fees wherever you go.

7.9 Accounting, reporting, tax and estate planning

Once again, I'm not an accountant, so this is just an overview from my point of view. Please see a professional for advice on your situation or any questions about specific tax and accounting issues.

Software

You need to track your business income and outgoings. This is mandatory if you have a legal company setup, but advisable if you are taking this seriously as a sole trader. You can buy accounting software outright, but I now use Intuit QuickBooks as software-as-a-service, which means that I pay monthly and access the accounts over the internet (with security of course). The bonus is that I can give access to my (remote) accountant, and they can see whatever level of reporting they need without me having to send reports.

One recommendation I have from using it is to decide on your chart of accounts early so that your finances are entered into the right categories by you or your bookkeeper from the start. A chart of accounts is a list of the accounts or 'buckets' into which you/your bookkeeper enter your transactions.

As covered earlier, I have separate income accounts for each of my income streams – book royalties, speaking, consulting, product sales, sponsorship, and affiliate commission – as well as separate expense accounts so they are trackable. Your accounts will likely be different, but it's worth deciding upfront how you want to split the reporting later.

Invoicing system

For book royalties and affiliate commission, you usually receive the money with some kind of statement. If you do public speaking, or if you sell books or products directly to customers, you may also need to use invoicing.

I have a simple template on Numbers (or Excel) and then save that as a PDF and email it to the Accounts team of whatever company I am working for. You can find these templates freely available in your word processing package of choice, or you can design your own.

Make sure to itemize as much as possible in the invoice so there are no queries, for example, travel expenses for speaking. Attach original receipts and keep photocopies if they are reimbursing you.

Be sure to include your banking details or PayPal account on the invoice as well as your payment terms, but keep in mind that many companies will only pay to their payment terms and not to yours!

The most important point with invoicing is following up the money if it isn't paid on time. I create a reminder in my calendar for five weeks after the invoice has been sent and then email promptly to follow up. I keep reminding every week until I receive the money. It's amazing how many large companies don't pay much attention to little invoices, but your cash flow is important to keep track of. This is a reason why I pay all invoices within a day or so of receipt, because I would like to be treated that way myself!

Physical filing system

A small business doesn't need a complex filing system, but it does need something. I use a plastic folder per month of the year into which I put all my receipts and invoices and paperwork. I keep bank statements for the year in another folder. Then I put all the folders into bigger boxes for the year over time, along with printed reports. Some people will scan everything into searchable form using Evernote or similar services.

You will find your own filing system over time, but just get it done and don't use it as an excuse for procrastination!

Reporting

In order to look at your financial reports, all of your income and expenses need to be entered into your accounting system, and reconciled to the bank account balances and on PayPal, i.e. the amounts need to match. You can then look at each of the transactions in the accounts to check that the detail is accurate and correct. Basically, the total amount in your account is not enough – you need to see how it breaks down. For example, income by distribution partner – Amazon, Apple, Kobo, direct sales, etc. Or expense by vendor name or type so you can see where you're spending the most.

The important reports are:

- **Balance Sheet**. This is a summary of your financial position made up of assets and liabilities. Assets include your bank balance, and may also include inventory (stock of books). It includes Accounts Receivable, which are invoices you have sent but have not actually received the cash for yet. Liabilities include tax owing, accounts payable (bills received but not paid) and anything else you owe.

- **Profit and Loss (P&L).** This looks at all of the income and expenses for the period, so you can see how the company is performing. Obviously you're hoping that over time, your income is higher than your expenses resulting in a profit. For authors, as for any business, there is an ebb and flow. So two months after a big launch, you may get an income spike as you're paid for those sales, and then you might have a dipped month if you haven't released a book in a while. This is also the report that you should use to examine your expenses in detail in order to make decisions on what you want to change in your business.

- **Cash flow forecast**. The ebbs and flows of your account can be tracked by forecasting your cash. I have generally done this separately on a basic spreadsheet by month by entering the amounts that are coming in as well as forecasting my average monthly outgoings. This is much easier when you're an independent author, as the publishing systems give you expected income at the end of a month, and you know that you'll receive the cash in two months' time. If you do a speaking event, you can usually expect to be paid in a month's time. This basic cash-flow is important if you are relying on your author income to pay significant bills like mortgage and rent payments. It's a critical tool if you're considering giving up your day job, as you won't have a salary coming in anymore.

Other metrics for your business

If you measure something, you can track it and make changes over time. If you don't measure it, you will make assumptions based on emotion and 'feel,' which may be wrong!

I'm not a data fiend. I barely look at my website traffic or my Amazon rankings. It's something I do occasionally, but there are people who track these things daily and tweak their business accordingly. (I am always keen to do my accounts, though!)

Here are some of the other regular measurements that might be worth examining in your business over time:

- Number of books sold

- Number of books in readers' hands – includes free books and giveaways

- Income per month

- Number of readers on your email list

- Number of reviews

- Number of books written or publications featured in, e.g. For poems, short stories

- Number of events spoken at

You need to decide how to measure your business, then revisit those metrics over time.

Accounting

If you have a legal business set up, you will need an accountant to help you prepare your taxes as well as your company statutory reports. I don't suggest you ever try to do this yourself, as you don't have the expert knowledge and there are better uses of your time. Your accountant will often earn their fees back easily by organizing your accounts in the correct way to enable you to meet your obligations and also optimize the things you can legally claim.

I work with a company that specializes in small business and I email them when I need to do my yearly accounts. I provide access to my QuickBooks online and email scanned copies of bank statements, PayPal statements and any paperwork they want to reconcile and check the accounts. By working with a bookkeeper who enters my receipts into QuickBooks, I minimize the amount of work for the accountant and pay less in fees overall. After the accounts are done, I sign them off and the accountant files them with the tax authority.

Tax

I'm exceedingly grateful when I pay tax because

A) it means I'm earning enough money that I have to pay tax in the first place!

B) I live in a country where I have police on the streets, a democracy, decent healthcare, free schooling and my streets are clean of rubbish. I have traveled enough in countries that don't have these things to know that I pay tax so I can have them. There will always be problems with governments but if, by an accident of birth, you're lucky to live in a country like mine, be grateful for it and happily pay your tax check!

Of course, I still have an accountant who makes sure my business is tax efficient so I'm not overpaying, but you should always make sure you put aside money for future tax payments. This can include income tax on behalf of your employees, as well as corporation tax on the income your business has made. I rely on my accountant to sort all this out, and they are also my tax agents, meaning that they deal with the tax authority on behalf of my business.

Withholding tax is a particular issue when it comes to authors earning global income.

If you self-publish through Amazon KDP or Createspace, Smashwords or Nook, and you're not a US resident, you need to sort out your US tax number and complete W8-BEN forms for withholding tax.

Yes, it's a pain in the a**, and yes, you have to do it or they will keep 30% of your sales and give it to the US government on your behalf. All the publishing sites have FAQ pages about it, and this article by indie author Karen Inglis is very helpful for completing the right forms - http://bit.ly/So1OTH.

You may have to do this even if you sign a publishing deal, as I have recently had to do withholding tax forms for German book royalties. It involved getting a physical stamp on certain forms, which has been difficult!

The key is to consider how much money you will NOT be getting if you don't fill the forms in. Sure, with one book and few sales, the amount may be very small, but over time, it may be thousands of dollars. There are two pockets – your pocket and someone else's pocket. So put it on the To Do list, put aside a couple of hours and get it done!

Estate planning

If you have children, you will likely have planned what would happen if you unexpectedly died. If you have assets and a company setup, you will also want to plan for this eventuality. Death is a certainty – the main question is when – so planning for the continuation of your assets into the future is important for authors.

Most will leave it until later in life, but if you are ready to get this sorted, I recommend checking out these resources:

- Kristine Rusch Estate Planning series of articles - http://bit.ly/1nXwYKU

- Death and the self-pubbed writer by J.A.Konrath - http://bit.ly/1rMVJkh

- What happens when an author dies at The Passive Voice - http://bit.ly/1t0I98D

Part 8:
Strategy and
Planning

8.1 Definition

> "A good strategy honestly acknowledges
> the challenges being faced and provides an
> approach to overcoming them."

> ### *Richard Rumelt,*
> ### Good Strategy, Bad Strategy.

Sometimes, we can get so bogged down in the weeds of words and tweets and blogs and comparing ourselves to others that we forget the big picture. One of the important aspects of running a business is taking time to step back and be more strategic about the business as a whole. To work ON the business, as opposed to IN the business, even just for a couple of hours every six months.

In this section, we go through strategic thinking and developing your business plan, as well as managing your time, developing professional habits, accountability, and the long-term view.

8.2 Strategy

Strategy is deciding what you want.

And what you don't want.

That second part is really important, and something many authors lose sight of.

It also shouldn't be too complicated, as you'll forget it otherwise! And of course, it can change over time as you and your goals change.

Decide what you want for your business

You can't be everything all at once. You only have a set amount of time and energy. Part of strategy is deciding on the focus for you and your business. Go back to Part 1 and revisit your definition of success and what you want for your life. Try to make that more specific so that you can continually narrow down your focus. For example, "I want to write for a living," can be reframed as "I will write thrillers and non-fiction for authors and make $4,000 a month."

Decide what you will do to get there

There are only a few major things that will lead to a successful career as a writer:

- Writing

- Getting the work out to customers – whether that's through traditional publishing or self-publishing

- Finding and connecting with readers

The trouble is, we get distracted by the latest thing, the newest trick, some quick win that might enable us to somehow beat the pack. We forget that it all comes down to writing, and more writing – which continues to be both simple and yet not easy.

Decide what you will say no to

You also need to decide on the specific focus for your business. There are many distractions along the path and even though something sounds like a great opportunity, you need to consider how it works in your strategy. If you only have a set number of hours, how will you spend them?

Here are some examples:

- You've written several romance books, but you really want to write horror and maybe something non-fiction on quilting. These books will likely appeal to different audiences, so you need to decide your strategy, for example, focus on one niche while you grow your audience and income, leaving the other books until later. Time is your greatest resource. Spend it wisely. I've been wanting to write a memoir on my travels to spiritual places for many years, but the project is on hold until I've built a big enough audience and my income is more secure.

- There's an amazing conference on next month. You know you will learn loads of cool things and meet amazing people but it's not related to your fiction goals. This is something I struggle with a lot, as there's a couple of conferences that I have always wanted to attend. World Domination Summit (WDS) in Portland every July attracts bloggers I respect and would love to hang out with. But it clashes with ThrillerFest in New York, and I am primarily a thriller author, not a blogger. I know that if I went to WDS, I would get excited about a whole load of things that don't fit into my strategy. I would be distracted.

- You really want to learn about how to utilize social media and you could spend the next month doing online courses on every single different one – should you focus on Facebook, Twitter, Pinterest, LinkedIn? Maybe one of those will be the magic bullet for book discovery. Maybe you should just do all of them … or maybe that's not your strategy. Perhaps you should just pick one and try to get noticed by your target audience there first, or maybe you should finish the book before you even start getting distracted by social media.

There are no right answers and it's your life, but you will need to correct your course almost daily if you want to reach your goals. We are all easily distracted by the latest shiny object, so decide, write it down, and stick it to your wall so you remain focused.

Get specific about the details of your strategy

Now you know what you want, and what you will say no to, you can articulate the details of your strategy. Here are some examples of what you might be writing down:

- I will write 5,000 words a week and schedule time in my diary to achieve this. I will write first draft material and give myself permission to suck. I won't re-read my work while I'm doing the first draft.

- I will plan my series in advance and write within the same genre to appeal to the same audience.

- I know I get distracted by Facebook, so I will only spend two hours on social media a week and I will log my time in order to measure it. When I write I will disconnect from the internet and turn off my phone.

- I will have a new book out by my birthday each year, and I will work backwards, setting targets in my diary to ensure that I get there.

My own strategic journey

When I started writing in 2006, my overall strategy was to become the British Tony Robbins, a self-help author and speaker, making my primary income through professional speaking, information products, coaching and books. My virtual mentor was Jack Canfield, through his book *The Success Principles*, which I still recommend as a fantastic guide to achievement. I discovered blogging and online product sales and went down that route for my business. I focused on networking in the blogging world primarily, attending related conferences and networking with big-name bloggers, learning more about online marketing.

Then I started writing fiction … and loved it. I also found that my introvert personality couldn't cope with too much people time; that speaking too much exhausted me and left me broken.

In 2013, I made the big decision to change my strategy to focus on writing books and becoming known for my fiction first, only speaking occasionally and winding down the online courses part of my business.

So, of course, you can change your strategy over time, as you change yourself. But one of the biggest lessons I have learned in my life is that time in the market matters far more than you think. Choose a path and keep stepping in the same direction and you will get a long way after a few years. The problem comes if you keep changing direction so you have to keep starting all over again. Read *The Compound Effect* by Darren Hardy, a fantastic book that really goes into this in more detail.

8.3 Business plan

Some people think you should do a business plan when you first start a business, but for authors, I think most of us realize that we have a business slowly, so the plan often comes later!

However, once you decide that your writing is a business, it is a good idea to at least put together a simple business plan. Writing things down can help you articulate much of what is in your head and help you to focus on what's important. There are a lot of questions in this book, rounded up in section 9.1, and working through these can serve as the basis for your plan.

The following structure is the one I use for my own plan, which I revisit every couple of months. The Book Download page has a basic outline for you to download and fill in.

www.TheCreativePenn.com/businessbook-downloads

You're welcome to use it as a starter template and modify it to fit your situation.

Every time I revisit it and make changes, I save a new version with the date in the file name and in the header of the document. Our perception changes over time, and it's good to see how our decisions change, too.

What is the why behind all this?

I start with a section on creative and lifestyle goals, and the drivers behind the work I do. If you don't know what the point is, then you will give up in the inevitable hard times. These should also be more concrete than just "make money." I used to say that I only wanted to reach a specific income goal, and my husband reminded me, "If you just want great cash flow, go back to being an IT consultant. You'll make far more money doing that."

He's right, I would make more monthly income if I went back to my old day job, but money isn't the (whole) point of this creative life. So my list has entries like:

- **Measure my life by what I create.** Do creative work that I'm passionate about, which enables me to bring new things into the world. Be proud of my body of work over a lifetime.

- **Freedom** from physical location and from dependency on one income source, from people's expectations. The ability to make a living from my laptop wherever I go.

- **Travel, learning new things,** personal development and helping others on the journey to creation as the guiding principles for saying yes to projects.

I also have some more measurable goals around income and health as well as providing for my extended family. This section is mostly about reminding yourself what the point is, so everyone's will be different and everything is valid.

Strategic focus

Strategy is about what you do to achieve your goals as well as what you won't do. This is my focus:

I write, publish, market and sell my own books and creative products.

That may look obvious and simple, but I've had to refine

this a lot, and it's helping me to narrow down my business focus. As more opportunities come along, you need to know when to say no.

Here's what this involves by implication:

- I need to spend my time only on things that serve that statement.

- I don't publish or market other people's books, even though I get asked to do so most days of the week. I am not starting a publishing company or a marketing company that helps other people. I write books like this that can help more people on a larger scale, as well as writing entertaining and challenging fiction.

- I am a professional speaker, but that speaking has to relate to my books and creative products so that it serves a marketing purpose as well as providing income.

- I like to help other people, but now I have books and audio that sell off the back of the blog, so The Creative Penn site, podcast, videos, etc. serve as marketing for my books. I've progressively cut down on selling courses as they are not evergreen, thanks to changes in technology and need upkeep over time.

- I am not a software company, so I'm not partnering with startups on selling software, although I am pitched for this every week.

Company setup, ownership and structure

In this section, detail your company name, how it is structured, e.g. Director, shareholders, etc. You can also note down any legal information or contact details in the event of anything changing, for example, in the event of your death. This isn't morbid, this is pragmatic! See the estate planning info in section 7.9.

Products and income streams

I've broken this section into subsections and detailed what I have in each, including an inventory of titles and series. If you list out your inventory, you can keep track over time. You can also track book sales figures here.

- Books (print, ebook, audiobook) – ARKANE series, London Psychic series, 'Day' novellas, Non-fiction

- Professional speaking

- Affiliate income – commission based on selling other people's products

- Product sales – multimedia courses

Pricing strategy

This will change depending on your business model, e.g. a non-fiction author with a profitable back-end consulting business might charge $10 for one non-fiction book and $5,000 for a consulting session, so there are pricing tiers.

My own pricing strategy has free first in series, then $2.99 novellas, full-length novels at $4.99 and boxsets and audio for higher prices.

Financial plan

This can be as detailed as you like. I include my target income, and then my monthly actuals to see how things are going. It's also good to break down what you need to sell to achieve your target income.

For example, 1 book selling at $2 profit x 100 copies a month = $2,400 per year

That's clearly not enough to live on, but you can see that if you had 12 books selling the same volume at $2 profit = $28,800. That's much healthier.

Then you look at authors like Barbara Freethy, who has 30+ books in print, ebook, audiobook formats and you can see how authors are making a good living.

If you break down your income goal into how many books you need at a realistic sales number per month, you'll know how long it will take to get there. Most businesses take at least five years to make a decent profit, so keep that in mind! You can also track income per book, which will help you recognize what is more popular over time.

Production schedule

This is covered in detail in section 2.7 and you can add that information into this part of the plan. I include the books I am planning to write for the next year, as well as focusing on the specific series I am working on. Top indie authors talk about the importance of a series and how the tipping point can often occur at three to five books. I'm intending to have seven in each of my series, as well as expanding my non-fiction books, so even if I don't know the titles I will add in *ARKANE Book #7* as a placeholder.

Ideas are not a problem, it's execution that's difficult, so having these written down helps me know what's next on my list before I get distracted by other ideas.

Team

The term 'self-publishing' in no way represents the reality of the professional indie author's life. My team list includes:

- Fiction editor

- Fiction proofreader

- Non-fiction editor and proofreader

- Book cover designer

- Interior book designer

- Graphic designer

- Audiobook narrators

- Virtual assistant

- Technical blog help

- Podcast transcriptionist

- Bookkeeper

- Accountant

Each of these is a named individual, and I have other roles for business accountability, beta readers and others that change more over time. It's worth noting down the roles that you also want to fill if you haven't settled on someone yet. For example, I am still looking for a sales data analyst who can help with my internal reporting, and help me with my royalty-split calculations.

Customers/ Target audience

In this section, I break down what characterizes my books and what types of readers would like each type of book. This was covered in Part 4 so revisit your conclusions from that and add them here.

Marketing and promotion

An outline of my marketing focus, as well as development plans. For example, when I started out with TheCreative-Penn.com, I didn't have any social media profiles, no podcast, no YouTube. I just started blogging. Then I added the podcast, then video, then Twitter, then the other social media over about 18 months. You don't have to do everything at once, but have some kind of developmental plan, or a monthly focus. This might be a rolling advertising plan, or when you want to make books free.

Niche analysis

Some people might call this 'competition,' but I believe more in 'co-opetition.' Identifying other authors in your niche, both well known and emerging, will help you with your categories on the book sales sites, marketing ideas and more. Spend some time in the Top 100 books for the categories you're aiming for and visit those author's websites, buy their books, follow them on social media. What are they doing that makes them successful? Add that research here.

Remember to revisit your plan

The business plan is not a static thing. It's a work in progress, as we all are. No one need see it either, so write it in your own voice, your own language. Update it when you change your mind, and remember to add why you changed your mind. Keep snapshot copies over time, and you will see how things have changed over the years of your author business. We're in this for the long haul!

8.4 Managing your time

Running a business takes time, and one of the most common questions is: how do you balance your time between writing and the rest of it all?

Two kinds of time

Yes, we all have the same amount of time in a day. We are all bound by the finite number of hours in our lives. But the energy we have available is not the same and I think there are two different kinds of time available to us as author-entrepreneurs.

Creative time.

This is when you have the energy to be at your creative best. It may take some effort to work out what it is, but for me, it's always the morning. When I had a full-time job, I would get up at 5am to write before work, because after work, I had nothing left. I was exhausted.

Everyone has different approaches, so pick whatever time is right for you. This doesn't mean that you can magically stream gorgeousness onto the page at that time every day, because creativity is hard work, with occasional moments of flow. But mostly, it's about getting your butt in that chair and writing words that you can later edit into something fantastic. So decide on a time and then make sure that you actually use that time to create something new in the world.

Down time.

This is the other time that is not taken up by your family or day job commitments, but it is time when you're mentally tired and can't necessarily create something new. When I worked full time, this was generally any time after work, or during any breaks I managed to snatch, plus evenings. This is the time you can use for marketing, networking with other authors, learning, or other things that are not direct creation but are still part of the business.

You have to make some decisions about how you want to use those periods of time, and indeed, how large they are.

How I managed my time when I had a day job

Over 13 years of being a business consultant, I started a number of businesses on the side while continuing to work to pay the bills. I started my author-entrepreneur business in the same way, and made some specific decisions to create space for growing a new career.

- **Moved to four days a week and gave up 20% of my income.** This is pretty hardcore, but it meant I could spend an extra day on writing and building my business. This was a serious career change move for me, but I was willing to invest in it. I had already spent eight years on other failed business ideas (see my book *Career Change* for more detail!), so I was committed.

- **Worked early morning, evenings and weekends.** Basically, all available time was spent on creating things and learning how to be a writer, doing courses on marketing and online business. I didn't have much of a social life, but I was so miserable in my day job that I was consumed with the burning desire to make this new life work. I had a very good reason to jettison everything else!

- **We got rid of the TV.** We still watch specific shows by downloading them, but it means you only watch around 45 mins that is actively chosen media rather than passively watching whatever comes on. This frees up a couple of hours per night, or even just one extra hour that you can use.

How I manage my time now I'm a full-time author-entrepreneur

The challenges are different when you go full time, but you still have multiple competing priorities for your time. It's easy to fritter the day away if you're not disciplined.

There's a sign on my wall that guides my daily progress: "Have you made art today?" That's my aim every day, and art might consist of new words on a fiction or non-fiction book, editing books in progress, planning a speaking engagement, or actually speaking, creating a value-added blog post, audio, or video. Essentially, creating something new in the world counts as my definition of art. Everything else – email, social, meetings etc. – count as running the business and those things are necessary and fun, but if I'm not creating, I'm not doing my primary job.

My best tool for time management is my Filofax diary: yes, a physical diary on my desk in which I write everything. It's planned about six months ahead and includes days in the library for writing, speaking days, and personal appointments. I also have a physical calendar on the wall with my daily word count. I monitor hours spent using the OfficeTime app on my phone which keeps me accountable.

Essentially, you have to decide on your goals and take control of your life and your time. You have to get organized. That's it. It's simple but, like so many things, it's not easy.

I realize that these steps might not be for everyone, but you have to decide what you want to achieve, and by when, and then consider what you will give up in order to achieve it. How will you make room in your life for building your author-entrepreneur business?

It's not easy, but then nothing worthwhile is. Luckily for us, writing is a lifelong career, and so is building your personal brand and platform online. Where do you want to be in five years' time? How will you get there if you don't make the time?

Consider some of the following questions:

- How do you spend your time now?

- When is your creative time and when are you tired?

- What can you potentially give up to make some room for writing and marketing activities?

8.5 Developing professional habits

There are books that we return to again and again for guidance as writers and creatives. I read *Turning Pro* by Steven Pressfield every new year, and often mid-year as well. I have the ebook, the print book, and the audio version on my iPod, and it's the only book I own in all formats. The main message is about how we can move from being amateurs to being professionals, and this attitude is what separates us from the pack.

Do you want to be a professional author?

Then you need professional habits.

I recommend you read *Turning Pro* for all the details, but here are some of my lessons learned that may help you on the journey.

"The difference between an amateur and a professional is in their habits. A professional has professional habits."

Pro writers write, and keep writing over time. The successful pro writers, like Pressfield, have multiple books that they continue to produce, even when previous book sales didn't perform as they would have liked.

Professionals aren't put off by short-term disappointment. They produce a body of work over time, and keep creating. They don't believe that one book is a special snowflake and give up when it doesn't hit the mainstream. They know that each page is a development in a journey. The habit is creating every day.

Distractions and displacement activities are the things that keep us as amateurs.

"When we're living as amateurs, we're running away from our calling – meaning our work, our destiny, the obligation to become our truest and highest selves."

Distractions might include blogging, Twitter and Facebook, when they aren't serving a business purpose. They are not inherently bad, they just distract us from our true purpose when we go down a rabbit hole on the internet, losing hours in the process, when we focus on watching what others are doing instead of creating our own art.

For me, this also means curtailing my public speaking engagements to a maximum of one per month so I have quiet time to write. In terms of 'fun' distractions, there's no harm in them. We all need fun. But Pressfield says, "Lives go down the tubes one repetition at a time, one deflection at a time." So watching one hour of TV a night still allows for creativity, but watching four hours a night and more at weekends so you have no time to create will stop you from achieving your creative goals over time.

"Resistance hates concentration and depth ... Resistance wants to keep us shallow and unfocused. So it makes the shallow and superficial intoxicating."

Have you checked your email in the last half an hour? Are you addicted to your smart phone or tablet?

One of the essential points seems to be that email programs, Twitter and Facebook should be turned off during creative time. There is no such thing as multi-tasking. It is only task-switching, which means that your depth of concentration is broken. Pressfield emphasizes that the Muse won't tolerate these distractions.

Here are a few of my tricks for focusing my creative time:

- **Take email off your phone,** which frees up thinking time and helps to curb the addiction!

- **Turn off all notifications** on your phone, tablets and computer. Set your phone to Airplane mode when you're writing.

- Use an app like Antisocial to **stop access to social media and email**. You can turn off your internet altogether if you like, but I often research while I'm writing. I just want to prevent 'accidental' glances at email and social networks.

- **Get your brain into a creative state.** Many writers use music – varying from classical to hard rap, white noise through noise-canceling headphones, or ear-plugs. I wear headphones and listen to rain and storms on repeat. It blocks out noise and also serves to get me into a certain head-state.

- There are no rules, but you need to find your own way to focus and go deeper into your own creative concentration.

"The amateur continuously rates himself in relation to others..."

"... becoming self-inflated if his fortunes rise, and desperately anxious if his star should fall. The amateur craves third-party validation."

OUCH. That hurts, because I definitely suffer from this 'comparisonitis' at times. I try to see other authors' success as an inspiration to try harder, but I sometimes fall into this trap. How about you?

When we turn pro, "we now structure our hours not to flee from fear, but to confront it and overcome it. We plan our activities in order to accomplish an aim. And we bring our will to bear so that we stick to this resolution. This changes our days completely."

I love this comment because it describes how professional writers get their work done. Their days are focused around writing, researching or aspects of accomplishing the aim that is the next book. This goal enables you to say no to things that don't fit with accomplishing it.

Turning pro is a decision we make every day.

I have this quote from Pressfield's *The War of Art* on my wall and I look at it every day.

"On the field of the self stand a knight and a dragon.
You are the knight. Resistance is the dragon.
The battle must be fought anew every day."

Every day we have to make the decision to be a professional writer. We have to write and not be distracted by the other things that call for our time. There will be days when we will lose. No one said this was easy! But over time, as we develop the habit, we will find ourselves winning more days than not.

Another one of my virtual mentors, someone who inspires me with their dedication to the craft, is Dean Wesley Smith. He has been writing in public for the last year, sharing his word count every day and being honest about what he does with his time. It's fascinating to read about his habits. He's a night owl, writing in the small hours and getting up late in the day. He naps a lot with his cat. He combines writing in spurts with visiting his publishing company office and doing 'real life' chores and seeing friends. But what shines through is his creation habit. Go check out the series here: http://bit.ly/1A6GjWu.

There are two rewards for what we do as professional creatives.

There's the conventional reward – money, applause, attention – which may or may not come. Then there's the psychological reward – the practice of writing and creativity that sustains us even if the conventional reward is practically nonexistent. We need to work for the latter, not the former. "Our intention as artists is to get better, to go deeper, to work closer and closer to the bone." Only our professional habits will get us there.

8.6 Accountability

Once you have a strategy and a business plan, it's very easy to put them in a drawer and forget about them!

We're all human – we all need to course correct. It's said that planes spend 90% of their flight time off the flight path and that constant course correction is necessary to get the final destination. We all need to constantly refocus, so here are some of the ways I use to keep myself on track.

Blogging, podcasting and sharing six-month goals in public

I've been blogging for over six years, and have shared my goals every new year and reflected on them every December. I also do a July review and reset, as well as talking about this in public on my podcast.

Having an audience, even a small one, can help you be more accountable to your goals. Here are my 2013 goals and achievement posts as an example of what you could do:

- Goal setting for 2013: Stick with Plan A: http://bit.ly/1tu5ljK

- End of year reflection on goals achieved in 2013: http://bit.ly/Wc3bqa

Accountability meeting

I have a couple of business-minded friends with whom I have monthly accountability meetings. One friend runs a completely different business and is not an author, so we talk at a level of products, income, and higher level business problems. We split the meeting into celebrating what we have achieved in the previous months, and then listing what we will do in the month to come. We also discuss issues around overwhelm, and management of time and people. I write minutes of this meeting to keep it official, and each month we revisit what we promised last time. It's fantastic to see how far we've come over several years of doing this.

I also have two author friends with whom I meet at least monthly, one in person and one online, and those meetings are less formal and more focused on what books we're writing and what we're doing to keep our profiles up in terms of marketing. There is a fine line between being supportive of each other, and then kicking each other's a** for not achieving enough!

Consider connecting with other authors at the same point on the journey as you and being accountable to each other.

Use virtual mentors as inspiration

I've never had an official mentor, but I have had hundreds of people I consider mentors in my life. Books are my primary mentorship, and I devour business books as well as non-fiction on writing, travel and psychology, as well as all kinds of fiction. I take notes in my Moleskine notebooks and try to apply the words in my life.

I also look to authors ahead of me on the journey as examples. You can read Stephen King's *On Writing* and then when you're confused about your direction, ask yourself: "What would Stephen King do?"

Actually, I can tell you what he would do. He would sit down and write! There are more of my recommended books in Appendix A: Resources.

Use the wall by your desk

I have a pinboard by my desk with a number of quotes and notes on it. Here's what's on it at the moment:

- Have you made art today? Have you written 1,000 words? Are you a step closer?

- Write to live. What is living today?

- What can I create today that impacts my long-term legacy and wealth? Weigh everything against this.

- Trust emergence.

- Pick yourself

- "On the field of the self stand a knight and a dragon. You are the knight. Resistance is the dragon. The battle must be fought anew every day." Steven Pressfield – *The War of Art*

These thoughts help me to focus every day. I need the constant reminder or I find myself doing things that just don't matter.

I also have a physical calendar on the wall where I log my word count. I don't write every day in terms of official word count, as I spend time in research and also editing phases, but this is a visual reminder of what I am creating over time. At the end of the month, I total up the words and aim to average 1,000 a day. I get a gold star on really good days!

8.7 The long term view

"Timing, perseverance, and ten years of trying will eventually make you look like an overnight success."

Biz Stone, **Twitter co-founder**

The biggest mistake any author can make is to think that one book will make you a fortune and provide financial freedom for the rest of your life. You will just end up disappointed. This myth of publishing success seems to exist in the collective consciousness, but is very far from the truth. The professional writer earning a decent living usually writes a lot of books and spends many years growing an audience. Even the lightning strike first book mega-hits often have an author with several unpublished books and years of writing behind them.

Everything takes time, but little steps every day will get you there eventually. But I know this is easy to say, and hard to think about!

So, here are a few things that may help you consider the long-term view of the author-entrepreneur business.

The future … Global. Digital. Mobile.

The last five years have seen a major shift in the publishing arena because of emergent technology and a changing economic situation. We've seen the rise of ebooks, the shift to online purchasing and the closing down of many physical bookstores, the indie movement with creatives selling directly to consumers, the empowerment of agile micro-business, the growth of mobile and apps and a global online economy.

With this pace of change, what will the next five years bring? The next ten? If you sell your rights now, if you settle for a deal where you no longer have control of your creative work, what will you miss out on over the next period of change?

It's too easy to get caught up in this book, in this month, in this year, focusing on how we can make money from one book and short-term spike marketing techniques. We're still enmeshed in a publishing industry and a media that is obsessed with the gatekeepers, with the traditional model of scarcity. But here are three game-changers that mean this revolution has only just begun.

Think global.

One of the reasons I love traveling is that it reminds me how insignificant I am on the face of the earth. It puts life in perspective, but it also excites me from a business view-point because there are readers everywhere. Walk along a street in New York, London, Tokyo, Lagos, or Delhi and you see potential readers.

People are people, regardless of where they live – they want education, entertainment and inspiration – and perhaps your book is the right one for them. Perhaps your book will change their life or touch their heart. English is also the most universal language, so writers who have English as a first language have a great advantage, plus the market for foreign language ebooks is growing every day.

We can now sell to anyone in almost every country with the internet. When I sold an ebook in Burkina Faso through Kobo I was delighted, and continue to tell people about it when I speak. Most people would struggle to find the little African country on a map, but someone there found my book and (hopefully) read it. I have now sold books in 58 countries – that is truly exciting!

There are readers everywhere, and more come online every month. The pool of readers is just getting bigger. Yes, the number of books is also increasing, but with more sophisticated discovery tools over time, authors can find a truly global audience.

Think digital.

I love print books and I believe that they will always be with us. But physical products, like books, require printing, warehousing and distribution. That type of infrastructure requires scale and favors the bigger companies and existing publishing houses.

But physical book buying, like many other purchases, is moving online. Print-on-demand technology, using digital files, means that we can compete selling physical books and products, as production and shipping can be done by companies that specialize in this technology.

Lots of online entrepreneurs now sell physical products without ever actually touching them or visiting a post office. Audiobooks used to be constrained by physical cassettes or CDs and now can be instantly downloaded. Digital commerce can be used for any products or services, and if you hold your rights, you can take advantage of any new opportunities.

Think mobile.

I mainly read on my Kindle Paperwhite at home and my iPhone Kindle app when I leave the house. I live in London with no car (like a growing number of the population) so I spend a lot of time on public transport. Reading on my cellphone is easy in cramped spaces, and I already carry it everywhere. Having a library of multiple books on the go is brilliant. I can turn pages, select new books and highlight passages with one thumb while holding onto the rail with the other.

I also live in a one-bedroom apartment and I don't have the space for thousands of physical books. When we moved here, I downsized my life and got rid of all our 'stuff.' My life is uncluttered and I want to keep it that way. In general, I buy knowledge, entertainment and inspiration when I buy a book, not a physical object. Going digital has increased my book purchases between three and five times. I am a super-consumer when it comes to books, but that is 99% digital these days.

I'm not alone in my choice of reading device or my attitude to digital. You may not read in the way that I do, but city dwelling, highly populated urban spaces, and smaller living quarters will only become more popular over time, and I'm typical of this growing percentage of the population.

Consider these macro trends and how they will impact the future of publishing and your author business. How can you ensure that you are ready to take advantage of new opportunities as they arise?

8.8 Becoming a full-time author. Why, when and how?

It's not advisable to give up your day job in order to write your first book and expect that book to make you millions, or even thousands of dollars immediately. I did this once and ended up going back to work a few months later, dejected by my failure. I didn't write again for five years after that, as my confidence took such a knock.

Of course, there are tales of authors who did do this successfully and thriller author Lee Child is probably the most famous. After being made redundant aged 40, he wrote his first novel in just a few months, sold it fast and went on to make multi-millions with the Jack Reacher series. But Child had years of working in television before that, so he had internalized what makes a story work and he wrote specifically for a commercial market. For most of us, moving to a full-time writing career is a slower process.

Do you even need or want to become a full time writer?

It's important to acknowledge that MOST writers have other jobs that pay the bills. You don't have to write full time, and it may be that you don't write the type of books that allow you to do so. That's fine. Some writers will spend many years on one book, and will need a job to keep body and soul together in the meantime.

Some people also love the work they do and don't want to give it up. In that case, writing books can be more of a beloved hobby, something serious but still on the side.

Revisit the business models for authors if you want to go full time, but don't be pressured into thinking that you have to make the shift because of peer pressure from other writers.

Evaluate what you need in order to go full time as a writer

If you want to make the jump, revisit Part 7, the financial section of the book and have another look at your projected income as well as the costs associated with the business of being an author.

Now consider what you actually need to go full time:

- **What are the financial outgoings of your life?** e.g. rent/mortgage, transportation costs, school fees, health, utilities and bills, food … and all the other things that we spend our money on. How will you handle those going forward?

- **What do you enjoy about what you do now? What will you miss?** For example, going from an office with lots of people to working home alone can be a major psychological shift. You need to think about your routines as well as your mindset.

- **How much time do you need to make the change?** What are the steps along the way? What are the milestones? For example, my milestone was that I had to be making $1,000 a month before I gave up my job. That way, I knew I could earn at least some money and that the business was viable and I could grow from there.

Minimize the risk of changing careers

I did a few things to ensure that my eventual move to full-time creative entrepreneur wasn't too much of a risk. These might also help you with your own transition.

- **I worked part time while I grew the business.** Basically, it took me four years to change careers, with very little risk along the way, as I built my business part time while paying the bills with my day job for four days a week. I swapped 20% of my income for that extra day, and I also worked weekends, evenings and before work to build my writing life. I worked a lot of hours, but as someone with a low risk tolerance and as the primary wage-earner at the time, it was the best way to do it after my earlier business failures.

- **I saved up six months' income as a buffer** for the move to author-entrepreneur, with the knowledge that those savings would pay the rent and bills if necessary.

- **We downsized our life from a four bedroom house to a one bedroom flat**, as well as selling the car. We got rid of all our debt, becoming location independent and lowering our financial risk profile. We made big lifestyle changes to allow for my career change and I can say that it has definitely been worth it! I'm also significantly happier without 'stuff.' I know that's not for everyone, but peace of mind around money is critical, especially in a partnership, and downsizing is one way to achieve it.

- **I encouraged honest financial conversations** with my husband to ensure matrimonial harmony! We were married in August 2008, when I was earning a high salary with a secure consulting career. When

I suggested moving to a totally insecure, creative model based around writing and speaking, my husband said "go for it," with the caveat that we would keep the financials transparent, and that my business would fund itself and not require top-up from our savings. I also promised to go back to the day job if I didn't make my targets – which thankfully hasn't eventuated!

What can you do to mitigate your risk of changing careers?

8.9 Looking after yourself

If you do choose to become a full-time author-entrepreneur, fantastic! Working for yourself is incredibly rewarding – you choose the hours you work and everything you do adds to your own asset pile, not someone else's.

But it's also important to remember to look after yourself, because the dividing line between 'work' and 'life' has just blurred, and you want to make sure that this will be a long and productive career. I'm writing this chapter for myself, as well as you, because it's something I struggle with!

Maintain and monitor your physical health

Headache and back pain, as well as RSI (repetitive strain injury) can be common issues for authors. The dangers of a sedentary job can also include obesity, Type II diabetes and other nasties. Some authors have moved to a standing or walking desk, others use speech-to-text software so they can walk or stand while working.

If you're sitting, set up your screen so you don't get neck pain, even if that's just by propping it up on books to get it to the right height. If you worked in a 'proper' office, you'd get this kind of ergonomic assessment, so don't skimp on your own health! Use meditation or mindfulness techniques to escape the crazy pace of the world, anything to keep your own peace. Make time for exercise – and remember, it boosts productivity and creativity too. I sit on a Swiss ball when I work, rolling around and leaning back over it to stretch and twist in mini-breaks. Before using the Swiss ball, I used to get chronic back pain that woke me up every night, but it's all good now! It doesn't matter what you do, but you need to do something. You won't be able to write if you're suffering from health problems.

Be aware of your mindset and your cycles as a writer

Originally, I had included the author's mindset as a separate section in this book, but it turned out to be so huge, I have separated it out for a different book. However, it's important to be aware that mindset plays a critical part in your happiness and success as an author, however you define it. For example, becoming consumed by jealousy about another author's sales, or spiraling down into doubt and anxiety when your story isn't working, will both impact your mental and physical health.

We all have cycles as writers, and as people. Our lives have rhythms, and part of looking after yourself is understanding how you work, and when you need some extra care. One of the signs on my wall says, 'Trust emergence.' It's there because I suffer huge doubts when I finish one book and I worry that I will never be able to write anything again. I know logically that my creativity ebbs and flows, but it feels as if I am empty and I will never be able to come up with anything new. That sign reminds me just to wait, to trust that something will emerge, and not to get too upset in the meantime.

Write down what you know of your ebbs and flows, your doubts and fears and jealousies. We all have them, and they won't go away, but we just need to be aware and not let them derail us for too long.

Make your working time efficient, and then schedule time off

Yes, you love what you do, but you also need to take time off. Most people can't actually work for more than a few hours of concentrated effort at a time, and then they need a break. If you do a couple of creative sessions a day, you will have achieved a great deal. Then take some down time. Read for enjoyment. Learn from other media like films and TV. Take a nap. Get outside and have some fun!

Life is for living, and you can write more from a richer life experience. I schedule regular international travel, as that's my kind of downtime, but also acts as research for my books. I also spend a lot of time reading for pleasure and I walk a lot.

How can you allow for downtime?

Take a digital Sabbath or use digital fasting on a regular basis

The fast pace of the internet and social media can drive us crazy. It can foster 'comparisonitis' – when you compare yourself to other authors, generally in an unfavorable way – and it can make you feel like you're not working hard enough, that everyone is doing better than you. You can also get distracted and go down Facebook or Twitter rabbit holes for hours.

A digital Sabbath is the idea of one day off a week, where you don't use the internet or social media and you don't check email – instead, you focus on family, friends, or just enjoying life. Taking email off your phone really helps with this, too! It's about being mindful of your attention.

Digital fasting can be an extended period of the same.

For example, I cycled through south-west India for two weeks and didn't check email or the internet once. It was marvelous, and I try to have a week off every few months now. The first day is the worst, as you feel yourself wanting desperately to check things – like a junkie wanting a fix – but after that, you realize that nothing is so urgent that it can't wait. After all, we're authors, and people won't die if we don't open an email or respond to a tweet today!

Basically, look after yourself and your business will thrive for years to come!

Part 9:
Next Steps

9.1 Questions to help you proceed

In this final section of the book, you can tie everything together by answering the questions that will help you move on. These questions are contained in the accompanying workbook, which you can access on the book download page **www.ThePenn.com/businessbook-downloads** along with extra resources and a business plan template.

Introduction:

What have you noticed about the rise of indie across multiple sectors? Has your shopping behavior changed in the same way mine has? Perhaps you can see the world changing too?

PART 1: From author to entrepreneur

What stage are you at on the writer's journey?

Are you an author-entrepreneur according to this list? Tick the aspects you already believe about yourself, and mark those you aspire to:

- An entrepreneur creates value from ideas, so I am an entrepreneur

- An author-entrepreneur loves business as well as art

- An author-entrepreneur turns one manuscript into multiple streams of income

- An author-entrepreneur cares about all aspects of business

- An author-entrepreneur is empowered

- An author-entrepreneur tries new things, accepts failure and pivots when necessary

- An author-entrepreneur invests in themselves

- An author-entrepreneur understands that luck plays a part

- An author-entrepreneur understands that the customer is critical

- An author-entrepreneur believes in abundance and generosity

- An author-entrepreneur has a long term view

What is your definition of success – for this particular book and for your writing career?

- How will you track and measure that success?

- What do you want to do with that success? What is the point in your work?

- What do you want your life to be like?

- What is non-negotiable?

- What are your core values?

Do you want to set up a specific company for your author business? Or will you run it under your own name as a sole trader for now? Why do you feel this way? What are the options in your company if you do want to set something up?

PART 2: Products and services

Do you understand what scalable means?

Write a list of your current products, including all the different formats your books are in. Now, expand that into the possible streams of income that could eventuate if you did everything covered in section 2.2. Can you see how valuable your rights are?

Which business model will you aim for? Or how will you mix and match aspects of them all? Which authors will be your role models and how do they run their businesses?

Evaluate your business model honestly. Rate each section from 0 to 10, where 0 is extremely unattractive and 10 is extremely attractive.

(1) Urgency. How badly do people want or need this right now?

(2) Market Size. How many people are actively purchasing things like this?

(3) Pricing potential. What is the highest price people will pay for this type of product?

(4) Cost of customer acquisition. How easy is it to acquire a new customer? How much will it cost to generate a sale?

(5) Cost of value delivery. How much does it cost to deliver this product?

(6) Uniqueness of offer. How unique is your product in the market and can people copy you quickly?

(7) Speed to market. How quickly can you create something to sell?

(8) Upfront investment. How much do you have to invest before you're ready to sell?

(9) Upsell potential. Are there related products that customers might also buy?

(10) Evergreen potential. Once the initial offer has been created, how much additional work will you have to put into it in order to keep on selling?

What are the most important clauses to watch out for when signing contracts?

If you have signed contracts, do you understand every clause? Do you know how and when to get your rights back?

What are your opinions around copyright, Creative Commons and piracy? Are you fully knowledgeable about all the aspects, or do you need to do more research?

- How many books do you want or need to write this year?

- How long does it take you to write each type of book?

- When do you need extra time in your plan?

- How much advance notice do you need to give your editor and cover designer?

PART 3: Employees, suppliers and contractors

What roles do you need in your current business? Do you have people in place for each of these?

As the author, what do you promise to the company?

What does the company promise to you in return?

If you want to write with someone else, consider:

- How will you approach working together? Do you share ideas up front? Does one person handle the outline and editing and the other write the first draft? Do you write alternate scenes? Who has final say on editing/cover design, etc? How will you split the marketing?

- How will you set up the contract for the split of the royalties? Who owns the copyright? If self-publishing, whose account will it be published from? Who will split the money and by when? Who has access to reporting?

- What happens if the book is optioned for a movie? What happens if you get offered a publishing deal for it? What happens if one person wants out of the agreement? What happens if one party dies? What happens if you end up hating each other? No one goes into a marriage expecting divorce, yet over 50% of partnerships do split up, so be very careful in setting your agreements up for co-writing.

What kind of editing do you need for your work?

Why do you want an agent? Do you know which contract clauses to avoid? How will you work with your agent/publisher? Have you discussed how it might end? Have you checked that you will get paid at the same time as the agent?

Are you interested in working with a translator? On what kind of deal? How will you work with them?

What decisions will you make around book cover design and formatting?

Are you interested in working with an audiobook narrator? On what kind of deal? How will you work with them?

Should you make a bookkeeper and an accountant part of your team?

If you are overwhelmed, what activities can you eliminate? What activities can you outsource?

What tools do you use to manage your team now? What might you need in the future?

PART 4: Customers

Know yourself. What are you interested in? What are your passions? What do you like learning about?

For non-fiction: What are the problems that your book is trying to solve?

What are the questions you are trying to answer?

For fiction: What are the themes and characteristics of your book?

What are the main aspects of the characters? What topics are covered? What can readers learn about? What places are featured? What themes crop up in all your work?

What are some similar books to yours? Who are the similar authors?

What category/ genre does your book fit into?

Who are your customers and what do they want?

Write profiles for your customers. Split them into different sub-groups if you have multiple series or brands.

How can you give great customer service and reward your customers?

PART 5: Sales and distribution

What distribution channels do you use for your books right now?

What distribution channels do you want to use in the future? How will you expand?

Where do you receive your revenue from? How many different sources? Is your business sustainable if that channel disappears or changes terms?

Do you want to sell direct? In what ways?

What names will you use for publishing? Do you want an imprint?

Do you want to use ISBNs?

What are your own pricing expectations as a reader?

How does that shape your pricing decisions for your own books?

How can you use various pricing strategies for your books?

PART 6: Marketing

How can you use these key concepts in your experience of marketing?

Attraction marketing, permission marketing, generosity, social karma, co-opetition

How can you optimize your book-based marketing?

How can you optimize your author-based marketing?

How can you optimize your customer-based marketing?

Who are your customers? What do they like?

What do they read? Or watch? Where do they hang out?

How can you resonate with your target audience in your marketing?

What are the aspects of your author brand? Do you need more than one?

Who is your target audience for these types of books, or this type of site?

Where do you want to be in five years' time? Can this brand grow with you?

How do you want people to perceive you? How can you communicate that in what you create in the world?

PART 7: Financials

What are your attitudes around money right now?

Do the income circles exercise:

- Draw circle/s reflecting your income sources right now

- Think about what your circles mean for you and your family. How much security is there versus risk in your income streams? What happens if your major income stream disappears or lessens? What are the downstream dependencies of that income stream, e.g. mortgage, school fees, health?

- Draw circles to reflect what you would like your income sources to be in five years' time

- Reflect on the differences between the two versions. Write down the reasons behind your choices for these future circles.

- What do you have to do to reach that future circle state?

What are your current revenue sources and monthly amounts from your author business?

What is your figure to be 'ramen profitable'?

- How long will it take for the business to get to this point? Do some projections based on your best guesses on book sales, profit and time.

- How can you increase your revenue?

What are the costs of your author business? How do you split out your expenses at the moment? How could you improve your tracking of expenditure by splitting them out further?

How will you fund your startup creative entrepreneur business?

Have you set up your bank accounts and PayPal account in order to run your business smoothly?

Have you done your tax forms and learned about your responsibilities in that area?

Have you sorted out a filing system and accounting software?

If you are ready for it, have you sorted out your estate plan?

PART 8: Strategy and planning

Have you thought about your strategy? What do you want? What don't you want?

What do you want for your business?

How will you get there?

What is distracting you from this core strategy? How can you refocus and correct your course?

Create your initial business plan using the downloadable template and section 8.3

How do you spend your time now? When is your creative time and when are you tired? What can you potentially give up to make some room for writing and marketing activities?

Do you have professional habits? Which ones do you need to improve?

How will you remain accountable to your goals and plan?

Do you even need or want to become a full time writer?

Evaluate what you need in order to go full time as a writer. What are the financial outgoings of your life? What do you enjoy about what you do now? What will you miss? How much time do you need to make the change? What are the steps along the way? What are the milestones?

How can you minimize the risk of changing careers?

How will you look after yourself as an author-entrepreneur?

9.2 Your next steps

> "The only thing worse than starting something and failing … is not starting something."

> ### *Seth Godin*

You don't have to give up your job to start taking your author business seriously. You don't have to have lots of books to begin to think of yourself as an entrepreneur. You don't have to have all the answers right now. You just have to be willing to learn and give things a try. Decide what you want for your business and get started. You'll figure out what else you need along the way.

A business is an evolving thing. Just as you change over time, so will your business.

What's brilliant about being a writer is that we can do this until the day we die. We can create, we can connect with customers, we can sell online to global customers with very little risk. It's a truly exciting time to be an author-entrepreneur! I hope to see you on the journey.

> "The best way to predict your future is to create it."

> ### *Peter F. Drucker*

Need more help?

If you'd like more help:

- **You can get the audio version of this book** as well as a video overview here: www.TheCreativePenn. com/businessaudio/ As you have bought this book, you can get a **$5 discount if you use the code: BIZCREATE** at checkout.

- I also have a **multimedia course** on *'Secrets of an Author Entrepreneur',* which includes video and audio interviews with New York Times bestselling author, CJ Lyons, whose indie books have sold over 1 million copies.
www.TheCreativePenn.com/prowritersecrets

- **If you'd like to learn more about book marketing**, check out *How to Market a Book*, which partners this volume. TheCreativePenn.com/howtomarketabook

- For more on public speaking, check out *Public Speaking for Authors, Creatives and other Introverts.* TheCreativePenn.com/speakingbook

- **For free bi-weekly audios** on writing, publishing, book marketing and creative entrepreneurship, check out The Creative Penn podcast on iTunes, Stitcher and SoundCloud.
TheCreativePenn.com/podcasts/

- You can also get your **free 87 page Author 2.0 Blueprint, plus info-packed monthly newsletters** by signing up at TheCreativePenn.com/Blueprint.

- **If you represent an organization or group** that the information in this book would be useful for,

I am available for professional speaking events. TheCreativePenn.com/speaking

- If you need **specific help** for your author business, I have limited 1:1 consulting available. TheCreativePenn.com/consulting

Finally, I always love to hear your comments and feedback, so you're welcome to email me: joanna@TheCreativePenn.com. You can also tweet me @thecreativepenn or join the Facebook Page http://www.facebook.com/TheCreativePenn.

Thank you

Thank you for joining me on the journey towards becoming an author-entrepreneur. I hope you've found this book useful!

If you loved the book and have a moment to spare, **I would really appreciate a short review on the site where you purchased**. Your help in spreading the word is gratefully received!

If you'd like to hear about the Mindset for Authors book, as well as keeping up to date with information on writing, publishing, book marketing and creative entrepreneurship, please sign up for the Author 2.0 Blueprint and newsletter at:

TheCreativePenn.com/blueprint

Other Books by Joanna Penn

How to Market a Book

Public Speaking for Authors, Creatives
and Other Introverts

Career Change: Stop hating your job, discover what you
really want to do and start doing it!

ARKANE Thriller series - writing as J.F.Penn

Pentecost: A power kept secret for 2000 years. A woman
who stands to lose everything.

Prophecy: The prophecy in Revelation declares that
a quarter of the world must die and now a shadowy
organisation has the ability to fulfil these words. Can one
woman stop the abomination before it's too late?

Exodus: A desperate race to find the Ark of the Covenant
– and save the world from a devastating Holy War.

One Day In Budapest: A chilling view of a possible future
as Eastern Europe embraces right-wing nationalism.

Day of the Vikings: A ritual murder on a remote island
under the shifting skies of the aurora borealis.
A staff of power that can summon Ragnarok,
the Viking apocalypse.

London Psychic series

Desecration: Death isn't always the end.

Delirium: "Those who the Gods wish to destroy, they first make mad."

Short story collection

A Thousand Fiendish Angels: Three short stories inspired by Dante's Inferno, linked by a book of human skin passed down through generations.
On the edges of horror, thriller and the occult.

www.JFPenn.com

About Joanna Penn

Joanna Penn, writing as J.F.Penn, is a New York Times and USA Today bestselling author of thrillers and dark fiction, as well as writing inspirational non-fiction. Joanna is an international professional speaker and entrepreneur, voted one of The Guardian UK Top 100 Creative Professionals 2013.

Joanna's award-winning site for writers www.TheCreative-Penn.com helps people write, publish and market their books through articles, audio, video and online products as well as live workshops.

Joanna is available internationally for speaking events aimed at writers, authors and entrepreneurs/small businesses.

Connect with Joanna online:

www.thecreativepenn.com/contact/
(t) http://twitter.com/thecreativepenn
(f) http://www.facebook.com/TheCreativePenn
Google Plus: http://gplus.to/JoannaPenn
http://www.youtube.com/thecreativepenn

Joanna also has a popular podcast for writers, TheCreativePenn.com/podcasts/

Joanna's fiction writing site - Thrillers on the edge: http://www.JFPenn.com

More information:

Joanna Penn has a Master's degree in Theology from the University of Oxford, Mansfield College and a Graduate Diploma in Psychology from the University of Auckland, New Zealand. She lives in London, England but spent 11 years living in Australia and New Zealand. Joanna worked for 13 years as an international business consultant within the IT industry but is now a full-time author-entrepreneur. Joanna is a PADI Divemaster and enjoys traveling as often as possible. She is obsessed with religion and psychology and loves to read, drink pinot noir and soak up European culture through art, architecture and food.

Acknowledgements

Thanks to Liz at Libroediting for her great edit, and to Jen Blood at Adian Editing for proof-reading.

Thanks to my fantastic proof-readers: Orna Ross, Jeremy Bouma, Mel Sherratt, Chris Grant and Alexandra Amor.

Thanks, as ever, to Derek Murphy from Creativindie Book Covers for the book cover design, and to Jane Dixon Smith at JD Smith Design for the print interior.

Appendices

Appendix A. Resources

This section contains resources for authors. You can download an extended version of this with hyperlinks to all the various resources and websites mentioned throughout the book on the Book Download page:

www.TheCreativePenn.com/businessbook-downloads/

Books

The Personal MBA: Master the art of business - Josh Kaufman

The Click Moment - Frans Johansson

The Success Principles - Jack Canfield

The Compound Effect: Jumpstart your income, your life, your success - Darren Hardy

Manage your day-to-day: Build your routine, find your focus and sharpen your creative mind - 99U Book Series

The E-Myth Revisited - Michael Gerber

The Freaks shall inherit the earth: Entrepreneurship for weirdos, misfits and world dominators - Chris Brogan

$100 Startup: Reinvent the way you make a living, do what you love and create a new future - Chris Guillebeau

The Copyright Handbook: What every writer needs to know - Stephen Fishman

Dealbreakers: Contract terms writers should avoid - Kristine Kathryn Rusch

Freelancer's Survival Guide - Kristine Kathryn Rusch

The Self-Publisher's Legal Handbook - Helen Sedwick

Choosing a self-publishing service - The Alliance of Independent Authors

Opening up to Indie Authors: A guide for bookstores, libraries, reviewers, literary event organizers and self-publishing, by Debbie Young, Dan Holloway and Orna Ross

Author, Publisher, Entrepreneur: How to publish a book - Guy Kawasaki

Let's Get Digital (How to self-publish and why you should) - David Gaughran

Let's Get Visible: How to get noticed and sell more books - David Gaughran

How to Market a Book - Joanna Penn

Write, Publish, Repeat: The no-luck required guide to self-published success - Sean Platt and Johnny B. Truant

The Bookstrapper Guide to Marketing Your Book: Creating a Bestseller By Yourself - Tucker Max, Ryan Holiday, Nils Parker

Influence: The psychology of persuasion - Robert Cialdini

Make Art, Make Money - Lessons from Jim Henson with Elizabeth Hyde Stevens

Art, Inc.: The Essential Guide for Building Your Career as an Artist - Lisa Congdon

Zen of ebook formatting - Guido Henkel

Making Tracks: A Writer's Guide to Audiobooks and How to Produce Them - J. Daniel Sawyer

Public speaking for authors, creatives and other introverts - Joanna Penn

Bird by Bird: Some instructions on writing and life - Anne Lamott

Writing Down The Bones: Freeing the writer within - Natalie Goldberg

The Successful Novelist: A lifetime of lessons about writing and publishing - David Morrell

On Writing: A memoir of the craft - Stephen King

The War of Art: Break through your blocks and win your inner creative battles - Steven Pressfield

Turning Pro: Tap your inner power and create your life's work - Steven Pressfield

Story: Substance, structure, style and the principles of screenwriting - Robert McKee

2K to 10K: Writing faster, writing better and writing more of what you love - Rachel Aaron

Story engineering - Larry Brooks

Rich Dad, Poor Dad - Robert Kiyosaki

Rich Dad's Cashflow Quadrant - Robert Kiyosaki

Virtual Freedom: How to work with virtual staff to buy more time, become more productive and build your dream business - Chris Ducker

Professional Organization for Indies

Alliance of Independent Authors: Global non-profit organization for indie authors with advice forums, teachers and advisors, online talks, contract advice and rights services. We're stronger together!

www.allianceindependentauthors.org

Writing tools and courses

Scrivener - the best and most amazing writing software ever! Couldn't do this work without it anymore :)

Write or Die software

NaNoWriMo.org

Courses

Skillshare - online training classes in business as well as art and design. I did a brilliant course with Seth Godin on The Modern Marketing Workshop. You can also check out Coursera, CreativeLive, Khan Academy, Udemy or iTunes University for free or cheap education on practically any subject.

Learn Scrivener Fast - great little videos on specific parts of Scrivener, so you can ramp up your usage quickly. http://bit.ly/Z7Jou7

Appendix B.
My lessons learned

Every year I round up my year as an author entrepreneur and share the details on my blog. Here are the last four years:

Sept 12, 2011. I am creative, I am an author. From affirmation to reality. I resigned day job and started my full-time author entrepreneur business. This article outlines my journey through years of not enjoying my day job, to my mindset shift and the final escape. I talk about what I will do on the site, including writing fiction and also doing more author training. http://bit.ly/1Bczjd6

Sept 12, 2012. Lessons learned from 1 year as an author entrepreneur. I am now earning the average wage for a UK female and my income split is 50% book sales, 25% speaking, 25% courses and consulting. My lessons learned are that it's easier to have a day job, but still absolutely worth it; I document that I have struggled with self-esteem and defining life without structure is a challenge and that you need a physical network as well as one online. http://bit.ly/1pr0bxk

Sept 26, 2013. Lessons learned from 2 years as an author entrepreneur. I am now earning around double the average wage for a UK female and my income split is 45% product sales, 42% book sales and 13% speaking. My lessons learned are that being an author is a viable business and the opportunities expand daily (the penny dropped around rights and multiple streams of income); time in the market and patience are key; relationships are critical for your mental health and your business, plus focus on what you love about writing and life. http://bit.ly/1bKcbr3

Sept 12, 2014. Lessons learned from 3 years as an author entrepreneur. I am now earning around double the average wage for a UK male and my income split is 40% book sales, 25% course sales and consulting, 20% commission/affiliate sales/sponsorship and 15% professional speaking. My lessons learned are that the industry may change but what we do doesn't – we just have to keep writing and getting our books to readers. Also, that if it's just about cash flow, go back to your day job, and that only by letting go of self-censorship will we truly find our voices. http://bit.ly/1qMVUK7

To be continued …

C. Tools I use in my creative business

You can download a version of this with hyperlinks to the various resources on the Book Download page: thecreative-penn.com/businessbook-downloads/

Warning: This list is quite long, but remember, you only need the things you need and I have added to the toolkit over the years.

Writing and Publishing

Scrivener. I've talked before about how Scrivener can change your life, but it really is my #1 recommendation, especially for self-publishing authors. It's amazing writing software, with brilliant drag and drop functionality so you can write out of order and then just switch things around later. But it also has a Compile function which means you can format your own .mobi files for Kindle and .epub files for Kobo, iBookstore and everywhere else. You don't have to pay a book formatter, and you can update your files with new books etc. All for just $49. Amazing. Try it here: www.literatureandlatte.com

If you're struggling with the amazing functionality of Scrivener, you can get lots of mini video tutorials with Learn Scrivener Fast. http://bit.ly/Z7Jou7

Wall calendar. Yes, it's a physical one :) I write my word count on it every day, and aim for an average of 1000 words a day in a month.

Publishing sites. Without these, many of us would still be in the day job!

- Amazon KDP for Kindle http://kdp.amazon.com

- Kobo Writing Life   http://www.kobo.com/writinglife

- Nookpress for Barnes & Noble Nook http://www.nookpress.com

- iTunes Connect for iBooks http://itunesconnect.apple.com

- Google Play http://bit.ly/1A2289D

- Smashwords http://www.smashwords.com

- BookBaby http://www.bookbaby.com

- Draft2Digital http://www.draft2digital.com

- Createspace http://www.createspace.com

- Ingram Spark (which uses Lightning Source and is aimed at self-publishers) http://www1.ingramspark.com

- Blurb http://www.blurb.com

- ACX - for audiobooks http://www.acx.com

Kindle app on the iPhone. I read like a crazy person and usually have 5-8 books on the go on my Kindle app, which I read on the Tube/ at the gym and anywhere else. I'm a research junkie as well as reading for pleasure, so my reading time is crucial to my writing life.

Business and productivity

Gmail. I love the new Gmail tabbed design that filters the emails I receive. Before that happened, I'll admit to being inundated, but now, all good :) I have it set up so I can email from my domain accounts, and use the settings to change my footers.

The smartphone. I have an iPhone 5, but I don't think the brand matters much anymore. The point is that you can work on the go. People always ask me how I find time for marketing, but basically I do things on the go. For example, I walked out the house the other day and there was a perfect rainbow in the sky. I took a pic with the phone, did brief editing on one app, and then posted it to Twitter in about 2 minutes. I count that as marketing of a kind as it gets some attention, which can lead into interest, desire and action, which is how social media really works. I'll also add that I took the email account OFF the phone about 6 months ago, and highly recommend it if you want to stop the stress and addiction of email!

Filofax. Yes, a physical one :) I schedule my podcasts months in advance, currently 4 months ahead, as well as meetings, events … oh yes, and personal stuff! I like having a physical diary and have tried to move it online but I keep going back to the physical. I actually bought the leather cover with my first consultancy pay-check back in 1997, so it has emotional resonance too.

OfficeTime app on iPhone. I keep a timesheet every day, which I learned from Sean Platt and it's been brilliant as it keeps me accountable every day. I have time codes for lots of different things, but essentially I monitor creation and income producing work against marketing and social things. http://www.officetime.net/

Things app on the iPhone and also the Mac. I have tried a LOAD of different To Do list applications but this works amazingly well for me. I also have a folder for fiction ideas, which I add stuff to every day. I know some people use Evernote as an ideas collector, but it never gelled for me. There was a documentary on Woody Allen where he showed his boxes full of one liners and ideas - well, mine is in the cloud! I like having it as an app and a desktop application as they synch on the cloud and I can add on the go and then check things off. https://culturedcode.com/things/

PayPal. I do a lot of business in USD and other currencies and Paypal has enabled me to earn income from anywhere in the world.

E-Junkie.com and Selz.com. These are the shopping carts I use for selling books and digital products.

Eventbrite.com. I've started using Eventbrite for live events and it is super easy to use for ticketing and online sales.

Mac Pages, Numbers and Keynote. I have a MacBookPro and use the suite of office tools every day.

Google Drive. I now use Google Docs for any kind of collaboration in documents as you can just share it. I also use the Forms feature which replaced SurveyMonkey for me.

Intuit QuickBooks accounting software. http://quickbooks.intuit.com

Website related

Wordpress. Just a few years ago you needed to know HTML or other languages to produce a pro website. But now you can DIY with what has been described as MS Word on steroids :) I use Beautiful Pro design on the Genesis Framework which is Premium design for both my sites.

Aweber. For email list management with scalable pricing that is compliant with anti-spam laws, I have found Aweber to be invaluable. Mailchimp is an alternative. http://bit.ly/1nxAqfe

Siteground.com for web hosting.

Multimedia

Skype with eCamm. Skype is free video or audio calling, and I use it for all my podcast and YouTube interviews, as well as talking business with my translators and other authors. ECamm records the video/audio, and if you're on a PC, try Pamela.biz instead.

Blubrry Powerpress Plugin for Wordpress. For streaming my podcast. They also have lots more resources. http://create.blubrry.com/

Amadeus Pro. For recording, editing and producing audio. You can also use Audacity, which is free. http://www.hairersoft.com/pro.html

Screenflow for Mac. For video editing and also screen capture recordings. If you have a PC, there are other options like Camtasia. http://bit.ly/1ikHX3A

Amazon S3 cloud hosting. Amazingly cheap cloud storage. I've been using S3 for years for all my video and audio hosting. http://aws.amazon.com/s3/

Social media

Feedly (http://feedly.com) **and Bufferapp** (http://buffer-app.com). If you follow me on Twitter, you'll know how many articles I share. About 80% of my twitter stream is scheduled, using these tools, usually from my smartphone in between meetings, or on transport etc. Feedly is an RSS reader tool, with a desktop and app versions. It integrates with Bufferapp which is a scheduling tool, so with a couple of clicks I can add content to the Twitter stream.

Tweetdeck on the Mac. For my desktop twitter experience :) https://about.twitter.com/products/tweetdeck

Camera+ app (http://campl.us) **on iPhone.** Really easy photo editing that you can then use as part of your social media marketing. I also use pictures a lot for research, and share all mine as Creative Commons Attribution Non-Commercial here on Flickr.com: http://bit.ly/1mFMRX5

On the iPhone - Twitter, Pinterest, Facebook, Instagram, G+, Goodreads. I do most of my social media on the smartphone, so have all the apps.

Appendix D. Money, Writing and Life. Interview with Jane Friedman

This interview was recorded in May 2014 on the topic of Money, Writing and Life. As the interview is quite long, it has not been included in the print edition, but you can listen to this interview in audio version and read a transcription here: http://bit.ly/1tv03Ex

You can also watch the video on YouTube here: http://bit.ly/Z7KaqV

Jane Friedman has spent more than fifteen years in the media industry as an editor, publisher, and professor. She's currently the Web Editor of the Virginia Quarterly Review, based at the University of Virginia, where she also teaches Digital Publishing and Online Writing. She's also the Editor of Scratch Magazine, which focuses on writing and money and life, which we are discussing in the interview.

Find her fantastic blog at www.JaneFriedman.com

Scratch Magazine: www.scratchmag.net

Appendix E. Make Art. Make Money. Interview with Elizabeth Hyde-Stevens

This interview was recorded in July 2014 on the topic of Make Art, Make Money - Lessons from Jim Henson with Elizabeth Hyde Stevens. As the interview is quite long, it has not been included in the print edition, but you can listen to this interview in audio version and read a transcription here: http://bit.ly/1naaYzK

You can also watch the video on YouTube here: http://bit.ly/1unheWD

Elizabeth Hyde Stevens is an award-winning fiction author, and she teaches fiction at the Gotham Writers' Workshop. She also created the Muppets, Mickey and Money research course at Boston University, and today we're talking about her book, "Make Art Make Money," which is absolutely fantastic, and I think should be required reading for every author who's taking this seriously as a business.

Find her at www.ElizabethHydeStevens.com

Appendix F. Q&A with editor Jen Blood

Originally posted as an interview on The Creative Penn, 14 July 2014.

What are the different types of editing that authors should consider?

In addition to the job of the final proofreader, there are three primary types of editing: Content, copy, and line editing.

Content editors are concerned with the big picture in your novel. Structural issues like plot holes, wandering timelines, character inconsistencies, excessive exposition, lagging pace... All of these fall within the purview of a quality content editor.

Copy editors do basic fact checking and help with the readability of your novel, ensuring that the prose is smooth and the style consistent. Line editors focus on punctuation, grammar, verb tense, spelling, and all those niggling things that drive most sane people mad.

At the end of it all, the proofreader takes your final, final, final manuscript and ensures that every comma, colon, and umlaut is exactly where it should be.

In most instances today, you'll be able to hire one person to do both copy editing and line editing for one price, and there are content editors out there who perform all of the above, though they are rare. Personally, I have a graduate degree in popular fiction and have spent most of my life deconstructing plot and pacing, so content editing is my specialty, but I've also worked for over a decade as a copy and line editor for traditional publishers, businesses, and individual authors. Consequently, I offer all of the above through Adian Editing www.adianediting.com.

What if I want an agent or traditional publisher? Should I get an editor then?

Absolutely! There will never be a tougher audience for you to try and sell your book to than an agent or publisher. Back in the good old days when publishers could afford editors for their authors, this was less of a concern. Today, however, it's up to you to present a publishable manuscript to the agent or publisher right out of the gate. A good editor is crucial to that process.

How do you find the right editor/s for your book? How do you know they're any good?

(1) **Ask yourself what you're looking for.** Do you just want a line editor to make sure you've got everything in the right place and you haven't made any egregious punctuation or spelling errors? Do you need a content editor who will address big-picture issues? Are you looking for someone who follows all the rules laid out in the *Chicago Manual of Style,* or are you hoping for an editor with a more creative flair? Are you hoping to learn something during the editing process, or do you just want to send your manuscript off for editing and be done with it? There are no wrong answers here, but you should have a clear sense of what your goals are in the process before you begin contacting editors.

(2) **Don't go to the yellow pages.** Rather than doing a general Google search, ask writers you respect whose work has been well edited for recommendations. Visit Writer's Digest (http://writersdigest.com/), the World Literary Café (http://worldliterarycafe.com/), or other popular writing sites, and visit the message boards there. There are frequently areas where editors can advertise their services. Keep in mind, however, that there is a difference between advertising on a site and being endorsed by them. Just because an editor is listed on a particular website doesn't automatically mean they are great at what they do. Due diligence on your part is still crucial.

(3) **First contact.** When you have two or three or five names of prospective editors, check out websites and contact them to find out if they are taking on new clients. You should receive an answer within two to three days at the most (remember—editors are busy people, too, but they should get back to you in a reasonable time frame regardless). Find out whether they specialize in content, copy, or line editing, what genres they are most enthusiastic about, whether they offer a sample edit, and—of course—what their rates are. Many editors will offer either a free sample edit of your first chapter or one for a small price, say $25.

(4) **What to expect.** During your initial contact with a prospective editor, don't expect them to wow you with some kind of incendiary insight into your work and how it's about to set the world on fire right out of the gate (though wouldn't that be nice?). Settle instead for prompt, courteous, professional responses from an editor who takes the time to find out a little bit about you and your

work. I have a standard questionnaire I send to anyone interested in my services, which gives me an opportunity to get to know the client and ensure that we're a good fit and our expectations for the process mesh. You want someone who shows at least a little bit of enthusiasm for you and your work.

(5) **What to look for in a sample edit.** If you are able to find an editor who offers a free or inexpensive sample edit, take them up on it. There are a few things you should look for when the sample edit is returned. First and foremost, is it back to you within the time frame the editor promised? Missing that first deadline is a giant, flashing red flag. Your editor may be the best on the planet, but if she consistently misses every deadline you give her, the experience is bound to be frustrating. Once you have the sample back, what kind of changes have been made or suggested? Does the editor offer insights you may not have thought of before? Does she give you a reason for why certain changes have been made? Is she enthusiastic about your work? These are all signs that you're on the right track in your quest.

What is the price range for editing? What should I expect to pay? How do I know I'm getting a good deal?

There is a huge price range for editing services these days, but in general for a quality edit you're looking at between .75 – 2 cents per word for proofreading, 2 – 4 cents per word for copy editing and/or line editing, and upwards of 2 - 6 cents per word for a good, qualified content editor. You'll want to find out up front if the cost includes revisions, or if you'll have to pay extra for the editor to look at your work again once you have made changes. As for whether or not you're getting a good deal, ask yourself what you hope to do with this novel. If you want your book to sell, whether to a traditional publisher or by publishing it yourself, how well do you think your unedited manuscript will do? A good editor can mean the difference between critical accolades and scathing reviews. How much is that worth to you?

I don't have much money and editors are expensive. What should I do?

Editors can be pricey, there's no way around it. If you're scraping the bottom of the barrel and just don't have the cash, look to your peers. At the very least, you need to have a circle of beta readers who will go through your work, and in exchange you can offer to do the same for them. Some editors—including myself—will offer a partial edit of the first few chapters of your novel for a reduced price, providing you with at least a starting point so that you have an idea what to look for yourself in the remainder of the manuscript. If you have a valuable skillset like graphic design, web design, or marketing knowhow, you might offer a bartering arrangement with an editor. Or, visit a nearby university to find out if there are any qualified students (or professors, even) who would provide an inexpensive proofread or copy edit. There are ways around the cost issue, so never let money—or the lack thereof—be your reason for putting out a subpar novel. You've written a book, the equivalent of running the marathon of your life. Hiring a qualified editor means the difference between you limping across the finish line or soaring past the competition.

What if I disagree with what the editor says? How much of their advice should I take on board?

Ideally, your editor is seeing your work after (or at the same time) you've had two or three trusted beta readers go through the manuscript. If, however, the editor is the first person besides yourself to read the novel and they return it to you with suggestions you believe are completely off the mark, you can do a couple of things. The first is to give the unchanged manuscript to the aforementioned beta readers. If they come back to you with the same suggestions, you'll know that your editor may have a point, much as you might not want to see it.

Then, ask the editor about the reasoning behind their changes. Is the story lagging? Was there a plot hole you forgot to fill in? Or do their changes feel more about stylistic differences related to your unique writing voice? If that's the case, it is a much more subjective issue, and I recommend making a list of the suggested changes with which you disagree. Then, talk to beta readers or fellow writers who know your work. Don't approach this as a b**chfest where you go off on the editor and your friends assure you that you're a genius. Instead, approach them with, "My editor has some changes I'm not sure about. Can I run a few things by you, and see if you've had similar reactions you might not have noticed, or if they're off the mark? I just want the novel to be the best it can be."

As for how much advice you should take on board, I don't know any author who takes every single suggestion their editor makes. The choice is yours with respect to stylistic changes, but hopefully your editor isn't doing a lot that you feel impacts your writing style, anyway. Simply look at the editor's reasoning behind some of the more significant suggestions they've made, weigh the validity of their argument, and then make your decision. We're not gods, we're just editors. You won't get struck down if you choose to pass on a few of our ideas.

My manuscript came back covered in red ink/littered with Track Changes. I'm really upset by the comments. How do I cope with the difficulty of being edited?

Okay, here's the sad fact: If your editor is not returning a manuscript covered in red ink/littered with Track Changes, you need a new editor. That's our job. Our number one goal is to make your work look brilliant. We aren't judging you, we aren't trying to make you look bad, and we certainly aren't saying your writing isn't fabulous. We're saying: "Hey, good manuscript—here are the things you can/should do to make it even better." Because that's what you're paying us to do.

It's hard to divorce yourself from the emotional element of producing this creative work, and to begin to view your novel as a product (I know—I used the 'P' word) rather than the flesh of your flesh. The editing process, however, is a great place to start doing that. How are you going to handle negative reviews from readers if you can't handle constructive criticism from someone you're paying to give it? Take a deep breath, recognize that all writers go through this pain, and try to listen objectively to what your editor is saying about your work.

With that said, you should never feel like you are being persecuted, diminished, or mocked by your editor. This is an important relationship, and you should feel first and foremost like your editor is in your corner. She wants you to succeed. She loves your work. She is enthusiastically plugging your books when they come out, and talking to you about your characters like they are mutual friends. You don't have to be BFFs who hang out online every day—in fact, chances are slim that that will be the case—but you should definitely feel a high level of trust and mutual respect. If that's lacking, it may be time to look for someone new.

Bio: Jen Blood is the bestselling author of the Erin Solomon Mysteries, and owner of Adian Editing, where she offers comprehensive content and copy editing services of plot-driven fiction, as well as writing coaching and classes on writing and self-editing. She has worked as a freelance editor for Random House, Aspatore Books, Hyperink Press, Maine Authors Publishing, and individually for a long list of independent and traditionally published authors. Jen is currently accepting new clients, with a few spaces available through the end of summer and into the fall. Visit www.adianediting.com to learn more about her services, or contact her at jen@adianediting.com to schedule a $25 sample edit of your first chapter.

Printed in Great Britain
by Amazon